Building Necessary Reading
And
Study Skills

Second Edition

Lawrence Scheg

This book belongs to :
Name: _____
Street: _____
City: _____ **State:** _____
Phone: _____
The information above is optional

Sierra Publishing
South Lake Tahoe, California

Maranatha

Ambiguous

ISBN: 0-9742756-6-2

Copyright © 2007 Professor Lawrence Scheg

All rights reserved. No part of this publication may be reproduced or transmitted in any form or by any means, electronic or mechanical, including photocopy, recording, or any information storage and retrieval system, without permission in writing from the author or publisher.

Requests for permission to make copies of any part of the work should be e-mailed to: ProfessorScheg@Yahoo.com

Published by
Sierra Publishing
1034 Emerald Bay Road
South Lake Tahoe, CA 96150-6200

Contact for Domestic and International Orders:
Send E-mail to: mailsierrapublishing@yahoo.com
or visit www.SierraPublishing.com

Printed in the United States of America

1st printing

Contents:

Chapter one

What Creates a Good Reader?

What is Reading?

Reading is one of the ways by which we communicate with one another, gather information, explore the world, increase our knowledge, entertain ourselves, and prepare ourselves for our future employment. While reading is not the only tool that we can use to fulfill these needs, it is one of the most useful and necessary tools.

Reading is important if we are to be able to explore the Internet, apply for a job, write a letter, read the newspaper, get a driver's license, do well in school, or do well in our chosen career.

Reading is more than just words but it starts with words. As beginning speakers, writers and readers we learned words, then we began to group those words into sentences, eventually we began to group those sentences into paragraphs. This process involved putting our words and thoughts in some order that would make sense to another person.

The reading process acts in a similar manner. We have to try to figure out what the author is trying to tell us. Sometimes the paragraphs make sense but sometimes we have to go back and look at the individual sentences or words to figure out the meaning.

Words, therefore, are very important in the reading process. We must have a good knowledge of words before we can interpret them in sentences or paragraphs. Also, we must be able to recognize those words rather quickly or we will slow our thought processes to just reading words and not thoughts. The mind must be able to create thoughts from the sentences and paragraphs that we read and reading too slow can hinder that.

Take an index card or ruler and cover up the bottom half section of this sentence. You can still figure it out! Your eyes only need to see the tops of the letters – not the entire letter to know what it is. In a similar manner, our eyes only have to see the tops of the letters in each sentence for the brain to know what the words are. You are therefore capable of reading much faster than you do today. It is mostly a matter of knowing the words so thoroughly that your eyes and mind can recognize them without much thought. That skill takes time to develop and it starts with learning vocabulary words.

Vocabulary and Spelling

I usually ask my students at what grade level did they have their last formal instruction in vocabulary. Then I ask my students the same question about spelling instruction. Write your answers here before continuing on.

Last grade I received instruction in vocabulary: grade _____
Last grade I received instruction in spelling: grade _____

Most of my students will answer that it was grade 3. That is a sad commentary on our educational system. If you received vocabulary or spelling instruction beyond that grade level, you are in the minority who did.

The unfortunate truth is that you need to learn an increasing number of new words at every grade level. In the grades following the Pre-Primer level (of 68 words) you need to learn *approximately* the following number of new words:

Grade 1: 320 words
Grade 2: 540 words
Grade 3: 850 words
Grade 4: 1080 words
Grade 5: 1140 words
Grade 6: 1200 words
Grade 7: 900 words
Grade 8: 900 words
Grade 9: 500 words

Grade 10: 540 words
Grade 11: 600 words
Grade 12: 600 words
First two years of college: 600 words
Second two years of college: 600 words
Master's degree: 600 Words

That's approximately 10, 970 words by the time most persons have "completed" their education. Some areas of study may even require a greater number of words to be learned. Most persons, for example, who are accepted into a nursing program, or other medical field, find the amount of technical vocabulary to be learned to be nearly overwhelming. Many students who drop out of those, and many other programs of study, do so because they lack solid a vocabulary background and the knowledge of how to learn new vocabulary.

Now don't panic! You can begin today to learn the words that will help make you a successful person. Scholars report that Shakespeare had knowledge of over 30,000 words. I suggest learning approximately twenty new words every week. Twenty words multiplied by fifty-two weeks equals one thousand and forty words. If done faithfully, you will accomplish much with seemingly little effort.

One of my fellow instructors has a sign on her wall that says, "Insanity is doing the same things over and over and expecting different results." It's funny, and it's true. You must make a change in your life right now or you will be in the same place you are now; five, ten, even twenty or more years into the future.

The first thing you must do is begin to thoroughly learn many new words. This book will not supply you with most of those words, but I have written several books that can help you to achieve your goals. Those books are: ***Conquering Often Confused and Misspelled Words, Building Necessary Vocabulary and Spelling Skills, Improving Essential Vocabulary and Spelling Skills,*** and ***Advancing College Vocabulary and Spelling Skills.*** These are available online at www.SierraPublishing.com. Each of these books contains several new words that are commonly used in our society at each of those progressive levels. Every book also contains a CD Rom that has printable study cards (with the word on one side and the definition on the reverse side), interactive puzzles, audible practice tests, and other items that you will find useful in mastering the words.

Spelling is important because through learning to spell the word, you become more familiar with the word and how it is structured. This makes it easier for you to recognize the word when you see it in print. Spelling has the added bonus of making you look more intelligent when you write. People who misspell words are often incorrectly judged as less intelligent based on their spelling errors.

What Other Skills Are Necessary to Becoming a Good Reader?

Another skill that is necessary to becoming a good reader is the ability to read thoughts and not just words. You must read fast enough to comprehend the thoughts in each sentence, then the thoughts in each paragraph, and ultimately the thoughts in the entire piece that you are reading.

I once knew a man who talked so slowly, that by the time he had finished what he wanted to say, his audience could not comprehend what he was talking about. The same is true if a person does not read fast enough. The communication is reduced to disjointed words that have little connection to one another. We must know the words that we read so well that we are able to read them quick enough for our brains to understand the thought and not just the individual words.

Beyond thoughts, you must be able to identify the point being expressed and any support that is given to further explain that point. Also, you will need to be able to follow the flow of the writer's ideas and separate facts from opinions.

From that point of development, you will be able to more successfully read the newspaper, a short story, a magazine article, a novel, or perhaps search the Internet. This textbook will help you to develop the skills necessary to enjoy those reading experiences.

HW

I. Write a short answer to each of the following questions:

1. Why is it important to learn new vocabulary words?

To improve comprehesion and communication
skills.

2. Why should you learn how to spell new words?

So you could apply them to your essay
or a writing project.

3. What should you do if you are taking a course and the instructor does not cover the new vocabulary with you?

Study on your own time and take
control

4. How important do you think reading is to your future financial success?

Very important

5. Write a short paragraph about why you either like to read or do not like to read.

Most of time I don't like to read,
because it seems mind-numbing. I also
loose focus fast when reading, specially on
an uninteresting story or topic. I also like
to read ocasionally if the story or topic
interest me.

II. From the list of suggested Internet assignments (in the Appendix section of this book) your instructor may assign the topic listed below, or another topic, to research.

Write that topic here: _____

Due Date: _____

Additional Instructions or Notes:

_____
_____
_____
_____
_____
_____
_____
_____
_____
_____
_____
_____
_____
_____
_____
_____
_____
_____
_____
_____
_____
_____
_____
_____
_____
_____
_____
_____
_____
_____
_____

Chapter Two

Vocabulary in Context

Introduction to Vocabulary in Context

Besides memorizing a large number of vocabulary words, a reader may use context clues to help figure out the meaning of a new word. B) There are four types of context clues that you should be aware of, and those four types of context clues are: synonyms, antonyms, examples, and a general sense of the sentence or sentences that make up a reading section.

The Four Most Common Types of Context Clues

Synonyms

A **synonym** is a word (or phrase) that is very similar in meaning to the unknown word. In most instances, it appears in the same sentence as the unknown word, but it may also appear in another sentence (usually) in close proximity to the unknown word.

Each of the following sentences contains a vocabulary word in italics, which has another word or phrase in the sentence (or sentences), which is a **synonym** *for that word. Underline the synonym for each italicized word.*

1. The pesticide was found to be very **potent**, and the scientist, who underestimated its strength, became very ill upon contact with it.
2. Jane dresses well and appears to be a very **affluent** member of society. She can also often be seen socializing with other rich members at the local Country Club.
3. What **criteria** should be used to judge the worthiness of a candidate for public office? Should honesty be one of the standards?
4. Carrying a weapon to school is **prohibited**. Also, drugs and alcohol are not allowed.
5. An old saying is that "you cannot force a horse to drink." In a similar manner, you cannot **coerce** a student to study.

Antonyms

An antonym is a word or phrase that has an opposite meaning to another word. An antonym is often signaled by one of the following words or phrases: **yet, but, however, on the other hand, in contrast,** or **conversely**.

*Each of the following sentences contains a vocabulary word in italics, which has another word or phrase in the sentence (or sentences), which is an **antonym** for that word. Underline the antonym for each italicized word.*

1. Most persons appreciate **innovative** ideas, yet often the old ideas work well too.
2. It took nearly one year after the 9/11 attacks on the Twin Towers for order to return from the **chaos**.
3. Jose wanted a **lucrative** job, but delivering pizzas turned out to be unprofitable.
4. Wendy wanted to move from the **sweltering** heat of the desert; however she was not happy with the frigid temperatures in Alaska.
5. In contrast to Sam's previous job where he was able to exercise much authority, his new position **restricted** him to the decisions of his boss.

Examples

In this situation, examples are given to help the reader understand the new word. Examples are often introduced by one the following words or phrases: **for example, for instance, such as, an example, one example** or **to illustrate**. Sometimes, an example may be given without using any of these phrases.

Each of the following sentences contains a vocabulary word in italics, which may have another word or phrase in the sentence (or sentences), which introduces an example for that word. Underline the introductory word or phrase (if one is used) and the example for each italicized word.

1. The Taliban were found to possess many *lethal* weapons, such as rocket propelled grenades, machine guns, pipe bombs, and missile launchers.
2. Deciding which automobile to purchase can be a *grueling* experience. I had to visit several dealerships before I was able to find an honest salesperson.
3. Many doctors believe that citric acid added to our food may cause *indigestion* problems such as heartburn or acid reflux disease.
4. One example of my brother's *eccentric* behavior is his collection of worn out gym shoes.
5. The *debris* left behind after the outdoor concert included beer and wine bottles, paper cups, food wrappers, and even shoes.

A General Sense of the Sentence or Passage

Sometimes you can figure out the meaning of a word by the other information that surrounds the word. This information may be provided anywhere within the passage. Most often it is in the same sentence as the unknown word. It may also, however, be found in other sentences. This is where a simple rule of three can be useful.

* The rule of three works like this: If you come across an unknown word, cover that word with your finger, next read the sentence that the word is found in. If you can figure out the word from that then you are finished. If you still do not understand the word, read the sentence before that one, read the sentence that the word is in again, and read the sentence following that one. Within those three sentences, you will often be able to figure out the meaning of the word.

Textbook Definitions

Most textbook authors are aware of the fact that students will often encounter difficult vocabulary in the reading of the text. Many of the words are referred to as technical vocabulary, which means that these words are unique to a certain profession, or take on a unique meaning depending upon the profession that they are used in.

A good example of this is the simple word disk. In Computer Science, a disk may refer to a 3 ½" floppy, CD Rom, or DVD. In Nursing, a disk may refer to a part of the spine. In Automotive, a disk will refer to part of the brake system.

Words that take on new meanings are often defined for the reader. Also, words, that would be new for the majority of readers, are usually defined as well. In Psychology, for example, words like id, ego and super ego would stump most readers so the text will usually define those words.

When an author wants these words to stand out, he/she will usually put them in bold, italic, or colored ink. The words will then be followed by a definition and often an example to help the reader understand them.

When an author takes the time to do that, we should take that as a clue to underline the word, and its definition, and put the letters "ex" next to any examples given. Next, we should add the word and definition to a study card, or list of words and definitions, for further study.

What Do You Do if You Still Are Not Able to Figure Out a Particular Word?

There are several things that you can do. You may ask someone else to explain the word to you. Another approach would be to look it up in a dictionary. A third method would be to look it up in an Audio dictionary (either from a handheld unit or from a computerized audio dictionary such as The American Heritage Audio Dictionary). Also, if you have a book that has an e-book component, you may use the e-book dictionary to look up the new word.

The main point to remember is that all of these techniques are available for your use, and that words not learned today, will not be known by you tomorrow, next week, next month, or even five, to ten, to twenty years from now. Mastering new words is extremely important to how well you are able to conduct your life, not only today, but also well into the future – your future.

I. **Three** things will be required of you for this lesson. *First*, in the following exercise, **circle** the word or phrase that indicates to you that a context clue is provided. *Then*, **underline** the word or phrase that helps you understand the word in italics. *And finally*, **write** on the line after the example, then type of context clue that was given.

1. Marci is a **bilingual** speaker who can speak both English and French.
   Type of context clue: ___B. general sense French___

2. Persons with digestive problems often have to eat **bland** diets consisting of items such as bread, potatoes, Jell-O, milk, and rice.
   Type of context clue: ___synonyme problem___

11

3. When applying for a job, a person should dress neatly, for an
   unkempt look will rarely impress anyone.
   Type of context clue: _____antonym press anyone_____

4. Too much sugar is not good for an individual, also, too little
   sugar can be very ***detrimental*** for a person who already has
   low blood sugar.
   Type of context clue: _____synonym sugar can be very_____

5. Many persons seem ***indifferent*** to politics, yet our leaders will
   help shape our future, so we should all be concerned about
   who is elected.
   Type of context clue: _____antonym_____

6. One of the best ***antidotes*** for hiccups is eating a spoonful of
   sugar. I don't know of any better remedy.
   Type of context clue: _____synonym_____

7. I wanted to discuss my son's progress with his teacher, but she
   carried on such a ***monologue*** that I never had a chance to
   express myself.
   Type of context clue: _____antonym had a chance_____

8. Many people are very ***frugal*** with their spending. I, however,
   have confidence in tomorrow being able to supply my needs, so
   I spend rather freely.
   Type of context clue: _____Antonym_____

9. Tonya was able to reach a ***sound*** conclusion after a careful
   examination of the data.
   Type of context clue: _____general sense_____

10. Negative people will tend to ***erode*** your confidence and cheery
    disposition.
    Type of context clue: _____general sense me_____

12

II. From the list of suggested Internet assignments (in the Appendix section of this book) your instructor may assign the topic listed below, or another topic, to research.

Write that topic here:

_____

Due Date: _____

Additional Instructions or Notes:

_____
_____
_____
_____
_____
_____
_____
_____
_____
_____
_____
_____
_____
_____
_____
_____
_____
_____
_____
_____
_____
_____
_____
_____
_____
_____
_____
_____
_____

Chapter Three

Word Parts: Prefixes, Roots, & Suffixes

Word Parts

Prefixes, roots and suffixes are examples of what are called Word Parts. These are letter combinations that have the same meanings when encountered as parts of various words. They can help us to figure out new words when we see them. There are approximately 150 of these word parts comprising from five to ten times that amount of words. By learning these Word Parts, you will be able to figure out many words that otherwise you would probably have to look up in a dictionary.

Prefixes

Prefixes are word parts that are added to the front of a word, or a root, or a root/suffix combination in order to form a new word. An example would be *post* meaning after. Words like postpone, postscript, postdate, posthumously and so forth would all apply to this definition. Be careful though, the English language can be difficult, and as the definitions of words can vary according to context, the definitions of word parts may also sometimes change. Postal worker, post office, and postal have different meanings from the prefix/word combinations mentioned above. In this sense the prefix *post* has a reference to mail and mail delivery. Usually exceptions like this will not occur, but it is good to remember that they may occur.

For example:

postpone	to put off until later
postscript	to write after the main part has been written
postdate	to date for a date beyond the current date
posthumously	after death

For example:

postal worker	a person who works for the post office
post office	a place where mail is processed
postal	having to do with the post office

Roots

Roots are a word or a combination of letters that have a particular meaning and to which either prefixes and/or suffixes may be added in order to form a new word. An example of a root would be *claim* or *clam*, which means to call. Words like proclaim, proclamation, exclaim, exclamation, reclaim, reclamation are all examples of a root taking on prefixes, suffixes, or both, which alter it while building on its original meaning.

For example:

proclaim	to call forth
proclamation	that which is called forth or has been called forth
exclaim	to call out
exclamation	that which has been called out
reclaim	to call back
reclamation	that which has been called back

Suffixes

Suffixes are word parts that are added onto a root or a prefix/root combination in order to form a new word. A suffix example would be *hood* which means state or condition of someone or something. We may have words like neighborhood, adulthood, childhood, or statehood.

For example:

neighborhood	state of being a neighbor
adulthood	state of being an adult
childhood	state of being a child
statehood	state of being or becoming a state

Some Very Useful Word Parts

By learning these word parts you will greatly increase your decoding ability for learning new words.

1. a, an = not, without

amoral	Not moral, without morals
anarchy	Without government
anemia	Without proper oxygen-carrying material in the blood
atheist	One who does not believe in God
atypical	Not typical

2. ambi, amphi – around, both

1. ambiguous	Having a double meaning
2. amphitheater	A theater that surrounds the audience
3. ambidextrous	Able to use both hands equally
4. ambiguity	Having a double or unclear meaning
5. amphibian	Able to live both on land and water

3. ann, enn –year, yearly

1. annals	Accounts of yearly activity arranged in sequence
2. anniversary	Yearly celebration of an event
3. annual	Occurring yearly
4. annuity	A yearly payment
5. millennium	A thousand years

4. ante -before

1. antedate	To date before
2. anteroom	A room that comes before the main room
3. anterior	Before in time or place
4. antecedent	One who, or that which, goes before in time
5. antemeridian	Before noon

17

5. anthrop - human

1. anthropologist	One who studies ancient human remains &cultures
2. anthropology	The study of ancient human remains & cultures
3. misanthrope	A person who does not fit in well with society
4. philanthropist	One who gives generously to humanity
5. philanthropy	Love towards mankind

6. ant, anti-against, opposite

1. antagonist	A person who works against another
2. antibiotic	A medicine that works against the life of a germ
3. antidote	A substance that works against a poison
4. antiseptic	A substance that works against a septic (sewer like) situation
5. Antarctica	Opposite of the Artic (North) pole

7. auto-self

1. automatic	Runs by itself
2. automobile	Moves by itself (under its own power)
3. autonomous	Self governing
4. autonomy	The right of self government
5. autopsy	Seeing for yourself the cause of death

8. bene - well, good

1. benefactor	One who gives generously
2. beneficial	Good for you or others
3. beneficiary	One who receives good benefits
4. benefit	A good thing
5. benevolent	Having good characteristics

9. bi = two

bicycle	a cycle with two wheels
bigamy	being married to two persons at the same time
bilingual	able to speak two languages
binoculars	two lens able to see at a great distance
bipartisan	able to work with both parties

10. bio = life

autobiography	a life story written by oneself
biodegradable	able to degrade (breakdown) the life
biography	a story written about a life
biology	study of life
biopsy	a looking at the life of a tissue

11. chron, chrono = time

chronic	occurring over time
chronicle	a written account of a time period
chronology	a logical time order
chronometer	a device used to measure time
synchronize	to set time pieces to the same time

12. circum-around

1. circumference	The outer surface of a round object
2. circumscribe	To draw a line around; create a boundary
3. circumspect	Watchful on all sides; examining all sides
4. circumstance	Standing around an event
5. circumvent	Getting around something through deception

13. co- together, with

1. coherent	Making sense; being together in speech
2. coincide	To happen at the same point in time
3. coincident	Happening at the same time
4. coherence	Easily understood because it is organized together
5. cooperate	To work well together

14. col- together, with

1. collaborate	To work together on something
2. collusion	To conspire together
3. collide	To come together forcefully
4. collage	To put together pieces to make a whole artfully
5. collapse	To fall together

19

15. com- together, with

1. commend	Bringing together praise
2. committee	Group of people who come together to work on a project
3. commotion	With movement or agitation
4. companion	Associating with another on a regular basis
5. complicate	With complexity

16. con- together, with

1. condominium	Joint rule or control
2. condone	Agree with
3. conception	Bringing together an idea or life
4. congenital	Being with a person from birth
5. contemporary	Being with the temporary (or current) things

17. cred-to believe

1. credentials	Papers that prove the truth of something
2. credible	Able to believe
3. credit	Money loaned based on the belief that it will be paid back
4. discredit	To state (or prove) a disbelief in someone or something
5. incredible	1. Not able to believe. 2. Almost beyond belief.

18. cor - together, with

1. correlate	Having a relationship with
2. corporate	Belonging to the body of a large business
3. corporation	A large business that had combined smaller ones
4. corps	A group of persons working together (troops)
5. correspond	To reply with another

19. dem - people

1. demagogue	A person who sways the people by oratory
2. democracy	Government of the people
3. endemic	Peculiar to a certain group of persons
4. epidemic	Spreading through the population
5. pandemic	Spreading through the population

20. di – not, away, apart

1. diverse	Many parts
2. diversion	A turning away from the usual
3. divide	Breaking apart
4. divorce	Dividing into two parts
5. divulge	Giving away information

21. dict - to speak

1. addict	Speaking to
2. contradict	Speaking against
3. dictate	to speak out
4. dictionary	to speak the meanings of words
5. predict	To speak beforehand of future events

22. dis – not, away, apart

1. disarray	Not in order
2. disaster	Not good according to the stars
3. disconcert	Not in order (concert), throw into confusion
4. discordant	Not in agreement (not in accord)
5. disease	Not at ease; not healthy

23. e - out

1. educate	To draw knowledge out; to give knowledge out
2. erupt	To throw out
3. eject	To toss out
4. emit	To give out
5. eradicate	To erase out

24. ex - out

1. excavate	To bring out
2. exclaim	To call out
3. exodus	To go out from a place or country
4. expel	To toss out
5. exit	To go out

25. fid - faith

1. bona fide	true
2. confidant	One you can truly share your thoughts with
3. confide	To have faith to share with
4. confidential	Shared with faith that it will be kept private
5. fidelity	Faithful to promise

26. gen - birth, race, kind

1. generate	To create or birth
2. generation	Common period of time shared by persons
3. genesis	The beginning
4. genius	Original thinker; originator of ideas
5. ingenious	Well conceived (birthed)

27. graph – to write, writing, drawing

1. autograph	Written by oneself
2. calligraphy	The art of beautiful writing
3. choreography	The art of making maps
4. geography	Drawings or writings of the earth
5. graphic	Clearly written

28. gram - to write, writing, drawing

1. cardiogram	Writings of the heart rhythms
2. diagram	A drawing describing the parts of something
3. epigram	A short (usually satirical) poem
4. telegram	Writing sent across a distance
5. monogram	One written (or embroidered) letter

29. log - speech, word

1. analogous	Bearing some resemblance despite differences
2. analogy	A likeness between things
3. apology	Something said in defense or regret
4. dialogue	Words between two or more persons
5. monologue	One person speaking

30. logy-study of

1. archeology	Study of remains of earlier cultures
2. psychology	Study of the psyche (mind)
3. ecology	Study of the environment
4. embryology	Study of embryos
5. biology	Study of life

31. mal-bad

1. malady	Disease, disorder
2. malaise	State of being ill
3. malaria	Disease caused by mosquitoes (literally means bad air)
4. malice	Ill will towards others
5. malign	Badly aligned

32. meter, metr-measure

1. barometer	Measure of air pressure
2. kilometer	1000 meters
3. thermometer	Instrument used to measure temperature
4. tachometer	Instrument used to measure velocity
5. metronome	Measures (beats) time for musicians

33. mono-one

1. monogamy	Married to one person
2. monocle	Eyepiece for one eye only
3. monolith	A pillar formed of a single stone
4. monopoly	An exclusive trading privilege
5. monotone	One unvarying tone

34. pan-all

1. Pan-America	All American
2. panacea	Works for all
3. panorama	Complete view
4. pantheism	All is God
5. panchromatic	Sensitive to all colors

35. path-feeling, suffering

1. apathy	No feelings
2. empathy	In similar feelings
3. pathos	Moving tender emotions
4. sympathy	Similar feelings
5. pathetic	Exciting pity or emotions

36. ped-foot

1. expedite	To put the foot out – make it happen now
2. impede	Put foot in the way – stop, slow down
3. impediment	Something that stands in the way
4. pedal	Device used by foot to create motion
5. pedestrian	One who is traveling by foot

37. phil- love, life

1. audiophile	Lover of music
2. philosophy	Study of life
3. philharmonic	Loving music
4. philosopher	One who thinks & speaks of life
5. philology	Loving words & studying languages and the people who speak those languages

38. phob-fear

1. hydrophobia	Fear of water
2. phobia	Unreasonable fear
3. phobic	Fearful
4. acrophobia	Fear of heights
5. technophobia	Fear of technology

39. Phon-sound

1. megaphone	Funnel shaped device fro amplifying sound
2. microphone	Device for capturing sound
3. phonetics	Pertaining to sounds
4. phonograph	Player of sounds using records
5. symphony	Similar sounds played together

40. Post-after

1. postdate	To date for a later date
2. posterity	To leave items for those who follow after
3. posthumously	After death; published after death of author
4. post-mortem	Examination of a body after death
5. postpone	To put off until later

41. pre-before

1. preamble	Intro part of discourse
2. precedent	Serving as example previous to current item
3. prejudice	Pre-judging
4. prerequisite	Required beforehand
5. prevent	To keep from happening

42. pro-forward, before, for, forth

1. proceed	To go forward
2. procrastinate	To keep from going forward
3. proponent	One who is for something or someone
4. provide	To give forth
5. provision	To provide for

43. re- back, again

1. recede	To go back
2. revise	To go back to and change
3. revive	To bring back to life
4. recession	To fall back financially
5. revert	To turn back

44. scrib-to write

1. ascribe	To attribute to
2. proscribe	To write out, to doom, to "write off as dead"
3. transcribe	To write over again; to make a written copy
4. subscribe	To write one's signature beneath; to enroll by signing one's signature
5. prescribe	To write or give medical directions

45. script – write/writing

1. conscription	To write or hold for military service
2. manuscript	Hand written document
3. nondescript	Not able to easily describe through writing
4. scripture	Holy writings
5. subscription	Fulfillment according to one writing their signature for

46. spec, spect - to look

1. perspective	One's viewpoint; outlook
2. retrospect	Looking back
3. speculate	To look into the future and predict
4. suspect	To look at as being suspicious
5. inspect	To look into

47. sub-below, under

1. subliminal	Under the surface
2. submerge	To put under
3. submit	To yield to the power of another
4. subservient	To serve as an inferior
5. subterranean	Under the surface of the earth

48. super – over, above

1. superb	Over most; first rate
2. superior	Higher in rank
3. supersonic	At speeds above sound
4. superstructure	A structure built above another
5. supervisor	An overseer

49. syn, sym - same as, similar

1. synonym	A word having the same, or nearly the same, meaning
2. syndrome	A group of symptoms
3. symmetry	Equal proportioned parts
4. sympathy	Feeling similar to another
5. symphony	Similar sounds playing harmoniously

50. tele – far, distant

1. telegraph	A device for conveying the written word at a distance
2. telepathy	Feeling from a distance
3. telephone	A device for transmitting sound at a distance
4. telescope	An instrument used for seeing at a distance
5. television	Seeing images sent over a distance

51. tort – twist, turn

1. contortionist	One who can twist body in incredible ways
2. distort	To twist the truth
3. tortuous	pain inflicted which makes one twist in pain
4. contort	To twist together
5. torture	To inflict pain which makes one twist in pain

52. tri - three

1. triangle	Three angles
2. trilogy	A story in three parts
3. trinity	A representation of God in three personalities
4. triplicate	Three copies
5. tripod	A device with three legs

53. ver – true, truth

1. veracious	Truthful
2. veracity	The state or quality of being true
3. verifiable	Able to prove as true
4. verify	To confirm as true
5. verity	The quality as being true

54. vid, vis – sight, see

1. video	Visual portrayal usually using film
2. videocassette	A cassette that reproduces visual images
3. videoconference	Conference made through using video
4. videogenic	Looking good on video
5. visual	Able to be seen

How many other word parts can you identify that comprise these words? Highlight, or underline, each word part that was not already mentioned above.

I. From the list of suggested Internet assignments (in the Appendix section of this book) your instructor may assign the topic listed below, or another topic, to research.

Write that topic here:

_____

Due Date: _____

Additional Instructions or Notes:

_____
_____
_____
_____
_____
_____
_____
_____
_____
_____
_____
_____
_____
_____
_____
_____
_____
_____
_____
_____
_____
_____
_____
_____
_____
_____

Chapter Four

Point & Support

Introduction to Point and Support

One of the basic skills that you must master is the ability to identify the point that an author is making and the statements that are used to support that point.

Many persons make statements about many things, but looking at how they support those statements is crucial to the reading process. If we take every spoken or written statement as being true and valid then we would be a very gullible person.

It is not enough to know how to read; we must question, dissect, and analyze what we read. Unfortunately, people are sometimes wrong in what they speak or write about. Some just make mistakes, some interpret the world incorrectly, and some are out to deceive us.

We need to question everyone and every idea that is put forth. One of the ways to do that is to identify the point being made and then look for the support that is given.

The **point** should be clear and well stated. The **support** should be logical, clear, adequate and relevant. By being **relevant** is meant that it truly relates to the point being presented, and being **adequate** means there is enough evidence to convince a person that the point is well supported.

Basically the person is making a point and providing support as a means of lending validity to that point. As a reader (or listener), it is our responsibility to make certain that the writer (or speaker) has accomplished that task.

Relevant Support

As stated above, the support must be relevant – it must relate to the topic. You must decide if each point really does relate to the topic, or if the writer has somehow strayed from the main point under discussion. If they have strayed, we need to note that weakness in their argument.

Adequate Support

How much support is adequate? Are three items of support enough? Are thirty pieces of support enough? Actually the answer is left to the reader. You must decide when there is adequate support – much like a judge or jury must decide during a trial which side is most convincing. You may be right, but if you are not adequate in your support, you may lose your argument - or worse yet go to jail.

More about the Importance of Point and Support in Everyday Life

Many times we will read controversial material and that is where these techniques need to be applied most of all. You must evaluate the evidence being presented in the form of supporting details, and you must weigh all of the support (evidence) given from all sides if you are to make wise, informed decisions.

Remember this, most people write from a personal point of view, or conviction. Writers are able to present many items in support of an argument, but other writers may be able to present many other conflicting items in support of their argument also. As analytical readers, we need to explore all sides of an issue, not just the side that agrees with our way of thinking, if we are to make intelligent decisions affecting all aspects of our lives. Reading is not just a tool, it is a skill, and it can affect every part of our existence.

Outlining Point and Support Arguments

A very good way to evaluate arguments is to create point and support outlines.

First, you should create a T chart. Then, you should label the T chart with the topic being argued placed at the top. Now, state the point being argued followed by the support being presented by each side. (If more than two sides are presenting evidence, then modify the chart to include more sides by adding to the columns.

Once you have created this T chart outline of each point of view, you will be better able to see the relevance and adequacy of the various points and support presented by each side.

An example of a T chart:

Point Being Made

Support given by Presenter A	Support given by Presenter B
1.	1.
a.	2.
b.	a.
2.	b.
3.	c.
a.	3.
b.	4.
c.	5.
4.	a.
5.	b.
etc.	etc.

By creating point and support outlines, we will have a clearer view of the support presented by each side. Your outline should also include minor and refining supporting details as well (see chapter 5 for more information on supporting details).

I. Identify the Point being made by writing a P on the line before the correct letter. Identify the support given by writing S on the line before the correct letters.

1.

_S_ a. Dark chocolate has antioxidant properties.

_S_ b. Chocolate reduces blood clotting.

_S_ c. Chocolate can trigger the production of nitric oxide which keeps arteries flexible and increases blood flow.

_P_ d. Chocolate has been found to have many beneficial properties.

2.

_S_ a. Sunlight is a good source for vitamin D.

_S_ b. Milk contains many vitamins and minerals including vitamin D.

_P_ c. Several sources may supply us with vitamin D.

_S_ d. Many vitamin supplements contain vitamin D.

3.

_P_ a. Politics often encourages prejudices.

_S_ b. Major Parties often speak ill of one another, but rarely speak
  good even if the other party has done something worthy of praise.

_S_ c. Political parties often pit men and woman against one another.

_S_ d. Race is often made an issue in political campaigns.

4.

_S_ a. Our neighbors like to get together for barbeques.

_S_ b. The neighbors' children are well behaved.

_S_ c. Everyone in our neighborhood is kind and considerate.

_P_ d. I feel very fortunate to have such wonderful neighbors.

5.

_S_ a. Bicycle paths can be used for commuting to work.

_P_ b. Most cities would benefit by increasing the number of available bicycle paths.

_S_ c. School children could ride to school using bicycle paths.

_S_ d. People would save money on gasoline, car payments, and car insurance if bicycle paths were more readily available.

II. Using magazines, newspapers, or the Internet, find an article that interests you. Read that article, paying special attention to the **points** being made and the type of **support** being presented. Finally, fill in the information below. Be ready to defend and explain your answers.

1. What is the topic or title of the article? _Vitamin D_

2. What are some of the points presented in the article?
Human Body needs Vitamin D to function
properly.

3. What are some of the details, which the author gives, that support these points?
Vitamin D prevents disease such
as cancer and high blood pressure

4. Why do you think this person wrote this article?
They want to informed people that
without enough vitamins it could
cause vital damage against your
body.

III. From the list of suggested Internet assignments, in the Appendix section of this book, your instructor may assign a topic to research.

Write that topic here:

_____

_____

Due Date: _____

Additional Instructions or Notes:

_____

_____

_____

_____

_____

_____

_____

_____

_____

_____

_____

_____

_____

_____

_____

_____

_____

_____

_____

_____

_____

_____

_____

_____

Chapter Five

Main Ideas, Supporting Details, and Implied Main Ideas

Introduction to Main Ideas

Many tests that we take in school, or in our place of employment, require that we are able to locate the main idea. Those in authority know that their students, or workers, must be able to identify the main point in what they are reading, or not much benefit will come from that reading. That person will therefore not function well in school or in their employment.

In order to understand what we read, we must be able to identify the main idea that the author is trying to convey to us. This is often a confusing area for students but it doesn't have to be that way. Actually finding the main idea is an easy task. This chapter will guide you through some easy steps in order to accomplish the goal of locating, and understanding the main idea.

The Three Step Process to Finding the Main Idea

Step 1: Identify the Topic

The first thing you must do when reading anything is to identify the topic that the author has written about. Is the topic about buying a computer, baking a cake, fixing your car, shopping for new clothes, or something else?

The topic could be almost anything. Ask yourself, "What broad subject does the author seem to be writing about"? "What general overall idea does the author seem to be referring to"? The answer to these questions will help you determine the topic of that selection. The topic will therefore be the main *subject* that the author is writing about, and it can usually be expressed in a few words.

Step 2: Identify the Main Point Being Expressed About the Topic

Ask yourself, "What is the main point that the author is making about this topic"? The answer to that question will be the *Main Idea* of the paragraph, (or sometimes even paragraph**s**).

In the examples above, the main ideas could be: I had a great time buying my first computer; I never realized that baking a cake was so much like a chemistry experiment, I'll never try to fix my own car again, and Shopping for clothes is never boring even when you're on a budget.

Now we just have to check to see if we really do have the correct answer to our main idea search, and that brings us to the third step.

Step 3: Identify the Information That Supports the Main Idea

Once we think that we have found the main idea, we should check ourselves by asking, "Do all or most of the other sentences, further support, explain, or give added information, that further develops the

38

idea that we've selected as the main idea." If they do support that sentence, then most likely, you have located the main idea.

Let's review this easy three step process

Step 1: Identify the Topic
Step 2: Identify the main point being expressed about the topic - that will be your main idea.
Step 3: Identify the information that supports the main idea in order to <u>confirm</u> that you have located the main idea.

Main Ideas and the Topic Sentence

Not all paragraphs have a topic sentence, but most paragraphs do. For our discussion, at the moment, we will assume that the paragraphs we are discussing have a topic sentence.

The **topic sentence** is the sentence in the paragraph that states the main point that is to then be developed. That main point, as we have seen above, is the main idea. Therefore the main idea and the topic sentence are the same. If you can locate the main idea, you can locate the topic sentence. Conversely, another useful way to locate the main idea is to identify the topic sentence.

Locations of the Topic Sentence

The topic sentence (or main idea) may come at any point in the paragraph. It may then be developed by the rest of the sentences in that paragraph, or even be developed over several paragraphs.

Examples of the Various Locations of the Topic Sentence

Topic Sentences at the Beginning of a Paragraph

It is very common for a topic sentence to be the first or second, sentence in a paragraph. This is often the way in which textbooks are written because textbook authors are usually writing in a style that is very direct and informative. They present a point, give support that develops that point, present their next point in the following paragraph, and give support that develops that point, and so forth. This style is very easy to follow, highlight, create notes from, and learn.

An illustration might help us to further understand this:

Example 1: The topic sentence (main idea) comes first followed by any number of supporting details.

Topic Sentence
Supporting Detail sentence
Supporting Detail sentence
Supporting Detail sentence
Supporting Detail sentence

Example 2: The topic sentence comes after an introductory or transitional sentence. The first sentence, in this case, would function to introduce the reader to the general topic to be discussed, transition the thoughts from the previous paragraph to the current one, provide background information to help you in your understanding of the new topic to be developed, perk your interest in a particular subject, or it may present a supporting detail.

Intro, Transition, or Detail sentence
Topic Sentence
Supporting Detail sentence
Supporting Detail sentence
Supporting Detail sentence

Topic Sentences at the End of a Paragraph

In this situation, the details come first, and the topic sentence (main idea) is presented last. Often these writers like to save their "punch line" for last, or build up to the main point that they are making.

Supporting Detail sentence
Supporting Detail sentence
Supporting Detail sentence
Supporting Detail sentence
Topic Sentence

Topic Sentences That are Placed Somewhere within the Paragraph

In this example, the topic sentence (main idea) comes somewhere within the paragraph. There may be any number of sentences preceding the topic sentence, and there may be any number of sentences following the topic sentence.

Intro, Transition, or Detail sentence
Intro, Transition, or Detail sentence
Topic Sentence
Supporting Detail sentence
Supporting Detail sentence

Topic Sentences at the Beginning and the End

Writers use this style when they want to bring attention to their main point a second time. They are emphasizing the importance of their main point, and want to make sure that we notice that point. In such a case, there is still only one main idea, but it is being stated twice.

Topic Sentence
Supporting Detail sentence
Supporting Detail sentence
Supporting Detail sentence
Topic Sentence

Another illustration of this style would be as follows:

Intro, Transition, or Detail sentence
Intro, Transition, or Detail sentence
Topic Sentence
Supporting Detail sentence
Supporting Detail sentence
Supporting Detail sentence
Topic Sentence

In this example, the introductory sentence, transition sentence, or details are presented first. Next a topic sentence (main idea) is introduced, followed by more details, and finally a restatement of the main idea in another topic sentence at the end.

A Few Final Notes on Topic Sentences

Topic sentences (main ideas), as we have seen, may be found at just about any location within a paragraph. The reason for this placement is according to the style of writing that each particular writer uses on any given piece of writing. Always remember to decide what the topic is first, then decide what the main point is that is being made, and finally check your decisions by asking if all, or most, of the other sentences in the paragraph further develop the main point that you have chosen.

Also, a topic sentence (main idea) may cover more than one paragraph. When it does this, it is often developed over two more paragraphs. The author may have so much information to present, that it would seem too long, and perhaps confusing, if it were all in one long paragraph. For this reason, and to make it easier to read, the author breaks the details down into two or more paragraphs.

Introduction to Supporting Details

We have just studied the main idea as usually contained in the topic sentence. Now we will become familiar with supporting details and their relationship to the main idea. We will see how all of these parts fit together and complement one another in a well written paragraph or longer piece of writing.

Supporting Details

Supporting details do just what their name implies, they support the main idea. Their function is to further explain, provide details, or give evidence for the statement made by the main idea or topic sentence. There are many levels of support that may be used to provide this information. The most common levels are discussed next.

Major Supporting Details

Major supporting details are those details that have a *major* role in helping us understand more fully the main point (main idea) that an author is making about any particular topic.

Minor Supporting Details

Often a writer wants to give us a more detailed explanation of what has been written about. The minor supporting details therefore further explain the major supporting details. Simply put, they give more *detail* to the topic under discussion than the main idea and major supporting details do.

Additional Refining Supporting Details

Most discussions of supporting details end with the discussion of major and minor details, but many times an author has provided us with another level. That level we will call, "additional refining supporting details" since it functions as a refining of the minor supporting detail. Its function is to clarify the minor detail. At this level

43

in the paragraph, the author is giving us a very detailed look at the topic under discussion. He/she has provided us with a very *refined* look at the subject matter. It would be unfortunate, and not very scholarly, if we were to ignore that very important level.

Implied Main Ideas (letting the details provide the main idea)

To imply something means to suggest it. **Implied Main Ideas** are suggested rather than clearly stated. In this situation, the details will suggest the main idea. There will not be a topic sentence, but there will be a main idea – although the main idea is only suggested by the details.

Supporting Detail sentence
Supporting Detail sentence
Supporting Detail sentence
Supporting Detail sentence
Supporting Detail sentence

To find the implied main idea we must follow the same steps that we followed in finding stated main ideas. Those steps are:

Step 1: Identify the Topic
Step 2: Identify the main point being expressed about the topic - that will be your **implied main idea**.
Step 3: Identify the information that supports the main point in order to <u>confirm</u> that you have located the implied main idea

In confirming the correct conclusion on figuring out the implied main idea, it would be wise to ***write out*** *what* we think is the implied main idea. Then you can see if all, or most, of the detail sentences further develop that idea. You have, in effect, written a topic sentence. When you do that, you are now able to check that sentence against the details as you would in a regularly stated main idea paragraph.

Outlining Helps Us to Clearly See How the Main Idea and the Supporting Details Fit Together:

Often we can get a good idea of the author's true level of knowledge about a subject by outlining the information given in their writing. Generally, the more complete the outline is, the more knowledgeable, and thorough, is the author's treatment of the subject matter.

A typical outline looks like this:

I. Topic or Sub-Topic (within a chapter)
    A. Main Idea
        1. Major Supporting Detail
        2. Major Supporting Detail
           a. minor supporting detail
           b. minor supporting detail
               i. additional refining supporting detail
               ii. additional refining supporting detail
    B. Main Idea
        1. Major Supporting Detail
        2. Major Supporting Detail
           a. minor supporting detail
           b. minor supporting detail
               i. additional refining supporting detail
               ii. additional refining supporting detail

Notice that most outlines will contain several levels as shown above. Each level will refine the information or knowledge in more detail. Outlines start with the most general information and each descending level becomes more specific, or more refined.

Outlining shows us the very specifics of the piece of writing. We can easily see how each item relates to the others. The complete outline always proceeds from the most general statement to the most refined. Each level is labeled and indented so that we can clearly see its various components and how they relate to one another.

As can be seen above, outlines alternate numbering and lettering, and start with upper case then move to lower case. To insure that you will have enough levels, always start with Roman Numerals (they are numbers even though we tend to normally view those symbols as letters), then capital letters, then numbers, then lower case letters, and finally, lower case Roman numerals.

Diagramming or Mapping

When we diagram, or map out, our ideas, we are creating visual outlines. To do that, we might use any shape such as boxes, stars, circles, and so forth. In doing this, we are using another approach to view the author's ideas.

An example of diagramming, or mapping:

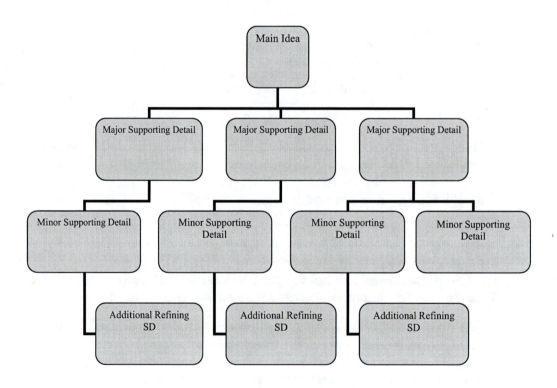

Let's apply what we've just studied:

I. Read the following selections, and then write the topic and underline, or highlight, the main idea.

1. _____ Digital Cameras _____
   Write the topic here

Digital cameras are very quickly replacing traditional film cameras. In the year 2003, more digital cameras were sold than ever before. One of the main reasons for this trend is the lower prices of the chips used to store the photographic images. Another reason is the large amount of photos that can be stored on one of those disks.

2. _____ Shortage of Bees _____
   Write the topic here

The lack of bees may be hurting crop production this year. Since many plants depend on bees for proper pollination, a shortage of these insects means that many flowering plants will not become fruit or vegetable producing plants. If this continues, we could experience food shortages.

3. _____ Rebates _____
   Write the topic here

Nearly every shopper appreciates a good deal. Few shoppers, however, take advantage of rebates. One reason may be that the shopper has to remember to fill out the form, cut the UPC code from the package, and attach the sales receipt. Another reason may be that they don't really need any of the products being promoted. But, the most common reason given is an indifference to the benefits of rebate items.

4.
_____ Santa Claus _____
Write the topic here

"Santa Claus is just a made up story," I've told my children. "Those gifts are from your father and me," I've admitted. "Christmas is a special time in which to remember the Christ Child," I've reasoned. You would think that my statements about Santa Claus would convince my children that he is not real, but, despite all the honesty welling up within me, each child becomes wide eyed with excitement when we pass the Santa display at the local mall.

5.
_____ Late Planting Vegetables _____
Write the topic here

Every spring, thousands of people plant vegetables that they will harvest during the summer months. Most gardeners, however, forget that late summer in several states is also a good time for planting. Vegetables such as cabbage, broccoli, carrots and lettuce may all be planted in a midsummer garden that will be ready to harvest before frosty temperatures arrive.

6.
_____ Killing Germs _____
Write the topic here

Many persons use aerosol products to kill germs in their homes. Often those products contain dangerous chemicals such as ethanol that the unsuspecting person inhales. But, there are safer methods of killing germs. One of those methods is hot steam. Pressurized steam cleaners are not as convenient as aerosol sprays, but they do kill germs and are probably less dangerous to your long term health.

7.
_____ Satellite TV vs. Cable _____
Write the topic here

Will cable television exist by 2010? With the ever expanding satellite television industry and the daily addition of thousands of satellite dishes to American rooftops it seems like cable television is certainly doomed. Satellite TV is usually clearer, often less expensive, and can offer true digital stereo sound. With all of these benefits, satellite marketers see the trend moving in their direction.

48

8.

_____ First Flight _____
Write the topic here

  In 1903, the Wright brothers flew the first manned and controllable aircraft. Shortly thereafter, many women made aviation history. In 1908, Therese Peltier of France was the first woman to fly solo. Bessie Coleman was the first licensed African-American pilot in the United States. Amelia Earhart flew solo across the Atlantic ocean in 1932, and was the first person to fly solo from Hawaii to California..

9.

_____ DVD Player _____
Write the topic here

As computer technology continues to evolve, the DVD player in your computer will become increasingly more important. Only a few years ago, we were impressed by the addition of the CD Rom drive to standard features of the typical computer. That was followed by CD Burners and now by DVD burners. Now, as some files (such as picture or audio files) consume even more megabytes, the consumer will find new software coming on DVD disks of 4.7 gigabytes rather than CDs of only 700 megabytes.

10.

_____ Automobiles _____
Write the topic here

Automobiles have wide consumer appeal. For one thing, automobiles allow us unbelievable freedom to move about. Another benefit is the ability to live at a greater distance from our place of employment than previous generations. Also, there is the aesthetic beauty of the automobile – so carefully designed as to entice nearly everyone into buying some make or model. Finally, there is the sheer pleasure of driving these often finely crafted works of art.

I. From the list of suggested Internet assignments (in the Appendix section of this book) your instructor may assign the topic listed below, or another topic, to research.

Write that topic here: _____

Due Date: _____

Additional Instructions or Notes:

_____
_____
_____
_____
_____
_____
_____
_____
_____
_____
_____
_____
_____
_____
_____
_____
_____
_____
_____
_____
_____
_____
_____
_____
_____
_____
_____
_____

Chapter Six

The Reading/Writing Connection

Introduction to the Reading/Writing Connection

You may have noticed by now that much of our discussion of reading also includes a discussion of writing. The two disciplines are often developed, and strengthened, at the same time. Many great writers were great readers to begin with, and many persons who become more proficient in their reading also find that their writing skills improve.

Thomas Jefferson read Greek and Latin texts from his father's library when he was only six years old. Jefferson was picked to write the Declaration of Independence because of his wealth of knowledge and great writing talent that had developed in part because of his reading skills.

Another famous writer was Frederick Douglass, who despite being a slave, learned how to read with very little help from society. Douglass fell in love with reading and grew into a great writer, statesman, and civil rights leader especially during the period surrounding the civil war.

All of the various skills discussed in this text will assist your writing development.

Let's take the knowledge that you have been exposed to so far, and let's apply that to writing.

First of all, as a person who is about to write something, you will need a topic. Next, you will decide what the main point is that you want to convey to your reader. The third item will be in the form of major supporting details to help further explain your main idea, and those ideas in turn will be further explained by minor supporting details. Finally, you might also want to add more information to further explain your minor supporting details which would be in the form of additional refining supporting details.

The following is an easy way to do all of that (there are more practice sheets that you may print out on the enclosed CD Rom.

A Reading/Writing exercise

The following writing exercise will help you to apply your knowledge of the main idea and supporting details to writing organization. As you do each step below, you may use pencil, and may erase, and change your answers at any step in the process.

First: Choose a topic, and write it on the topic line on the next page.

Second: Write a topic sentence (main idea) about that topic on the lines following Roman numeral I.

Third: After each capital letter, write **one word** that will further explain or expand upon your main idea statement.

Fourth: Now, after each number, write **one word** that will further explain each major supporting detail.

PARAGRAPH / ESSAY ORGANIZATION   *STEP 1*
(Outline Page)

_____
Topic

I.   **MAIN IDEA (TOPIC SENTENCE OR THESIS):**

_____

_____

_____

_____

    A _____

       1 _____

       2 _____

       3 _____

    B _____

       1 _____

       2 _____

       3 _____

    C _____

       1 _____

       2 _____

       3 _____

    D _____

       1 _____

       2 _____

       3 _____

If you followed the four steps presented on the previous page, you have created an **outline** for an essay. Now, on the next page, repeat steps one and two. Then for steps three and four, write **complete sentences** for each word idea from the previous page. When you complete this exercise, you will have created a rough draft for an essay. Simply copy the topic, topic sentence, and supporting sentences over to your computer, word processor, or paper. The final steps will involve rereading your essay and refining it. You are well on your way to a *well órganized* essay.

PARAGRAPH / ESSAY ORGANIZATION   STEP 2

_____
TOPIC

I. MAIN IDEA (TOPIC SENTENCE OR THESIS):

_____
_____
_____

   A. MAJOR SUPPORTING DETAIL (REASON #1):

_____
_____
_____

      1) MINOR SUPPORTING DETAIL:

_____
_____

      2) MINOR SUPPORTING DETAIL:

_____
_____
_____

      3) MINOR SUPPORTING DETAIL:

_____
_____
_____

B. MAJOR SUPPORTING DETAIL (REASON # 2):

_____
_____
_____

    1) MINOR SUPPORTING DETAIL:

_____
_____
_____

    2) MINOR SUPPORTING DETAIL:

_____
_____
_____

    3) MINOR SUPPORTING DETAIL:

_____
_____

C. MAJOR SUPPORTING DETAIL (REASON # 3):

_____
_____
_____

    1) MINOR SUPPORTING DETAIL:

_____
_____
_____

    2) MINOR SUPPORTING DETAIL:

_____
_____
_____

    3) MINOR SUPPORTING DETAIL:

_____
_____
_____

D. MAJOR SUPPORTING DETAIL (REASON #4)

-OR-

CONCLUDING SENTENCE(S) OR PARAGRAPH

_____
_____
_____

1) MINOR SUPPORTING DETAIL:

_____
_____
_____

2) MINOR SUPPORTING DETAIL:

_____
_____
_____

3) MINOR SUPPORTING DETAIL:

_____
_____
_____

As you become proficient at writing essays, these steps will automatically take place in your mind. Until that time, however, this approach can help get you organized, help get your ideas flowing, and provide more fullness to your writing.

I hope that by doing this exercise, you will more clearly see the connection between reading and writing. Also, I hope that you will realize that every good writer starts with a topic and then proceeds to present that material to the reader in an organized fashion so that it is clear and easily understood.

An outline helps the writer to organize the presentation of material to the reader. Conversely, an outline of a writer's work can help us to see the information as the writer first constructed it in its most basic form.

I. From the list of suggested Internet assignments (in the Appendix section of this book) your instructor may assign the topic listed below, or another topic, to research.

Write that topic here: _____

Due Date: _____

Additional Instructions or Notes:

_____
_____
_____
_____
_____
_____
_____
_____
_____
_____
_____
_____
_____
_____
_____
_____
_____
_____
_____
_____
_____
_____
_____
_____
_____
_____
_____
_____
_____

The PROCTRM Study Method

I. *Introduction to the PROCTRM Study Method*

I had just completed my BA degree, recently married, landed my first teaching job, and was about to enter graduate school. As I looked towards the future, I also looked back at the past. My grades were good, but they weren't great. I wanted to do much better in the future. I wanted to impress my parents like my older brother and sister had. My brother had become a doctor of optometry, and my sister had become a lawyer.

What could I do to impress my parents? An idea jumped out at me – achieve an "A" average in graduate school. That would certainly impress them! But now reality set in – how would I be able to do that? My health wasn't the greatest. In fact, I had to drop three classes, and take a few months off for recuperation, during my undergraduate studies. I could study harder, maybe even study longer, but would that achieve the results that I wanted? I didn't think it would.

Next, I thought, "Okay, what has worked and what hasn't worked so far." I knew I needed to not study more, but more efficiently. I began to sort out what those things were in my mind. Then, as I began graduate school, I started to apply them. The result was that I achieved my goal of an "A" average, despite another illness and a divorce during that period.

Most students are never taught a study skills method. Others are taught methods that don't really work. I taught at the high school level for eight years and then I was involved in several other careers for fifteen more years. In 1995, I returned to teaching – but this time at the junior college level. One of my first assignments was to teach my students how to study. I looked at the various techniques that were presented in the textbook and realized that none of them really worked.

I couldn't teach my students something that didn't work so I sat down and thought back to what had worked for me during my graduate school studies. I wrote that down and taught it to my classes that very day. The technique worked as well for them as it had for me.

The PROCTRM Method Explained:

There are *six* easy steps to the PROCTRM technique:
- **Preview**
- **Read**
- **Outline**
- **Critical Thinking**
- **Review**
- **Memorize**

These steps must be faithfully followed and applied, although some slight adjustment may be necessary as you encounter different textbook styles.

Step 1: Preview

When you preview a chapter, you get a good idea of the direction that the chapter will go. It's similar to going on a trip across the country. Perhaps you want to travel from Los Angeles to New York City. The first thing you should do is to take out a map and study the routes that will take you there.

Not everyone would look at a map before starting out. Some would be successful in traveling across the country in that manner, but most would get lost to some degree or another. The wise thing would be to study a map. Route 10 starts out in Los Angeles (and travels east for hundreds of miles) but you must connect with other routes in order to successfully arrive in New York. If you were to just continue on route 10, you might eventually end up in Louisiana or Florida.

Chapters in your textbook need to be previewed so that you have a clear idea of where the author is taking you - right from the beginning. Too many people just start at the first line of print and begin to read with no idea where the chapter is going, or what will be covered in that chapter. By the end of the first page, many people have daydreamed, thought of other things to do,
thought of their friends, thought of television programs that they want to see, and so forth. They have little idea of where they are going, where they have been, or why they are reading the chapter – other than that it was assigned by their instructor.

A preview of the chapter will erase many of those initial problems. Here is how to preview a chapter:

1. Open the text to the chapter that you want to learn.
2. Read the title, and then study every bold heading in the chapter, every chart, map, graph, picture, and caption.
3. Label all the Major chapter headings with Roman numerals.

These are Roman Numerals:

1 = I	11 = XI
2 = II	12 = XII
3 = III	13 = XIII
4 = IV	14 = XIV
5 = V	15 = XV
6 = VI	16 = XVI
7 = VII	17 = XVII
8 = VIII	18 = XVIII
9 = IX	19 = XIX
10 = X	20 = XX

4. Now, using Roman numerals, list, on your PROCTRM notepaper (as supplied on the CD Rom included with this text and shown below) the topics to be covered in this chapter.

Chapter 7 as an example:

ADDITIONAL NOTES, VOCABULARY DEFINITIONS, EXAMPLES, EXPLANATIONS, POSSIBLE EXAM QUESTIONS, OR QUESTIONS THAT NEED CLARIFICATION, ETC.	Name: Date: Class: Day: Time: **The PROCTRM Study Technique** **Chapter 7**
	I.) Introduction to the PROCTRM Study Technique
	II.) The PROCTRM Study Technique Explained
	III.) Review of the PROCTRM technique

5. This now should give you a clear idea of the direction that the chapter will take.

6. The next step is to fill in the details. A chapter might look something like this:

ADDITIONAL NOTES, VOCABULARY DEFINITIONS, EXAMPLES, EXPLANATIONS, POSSIBLE EXAM QUESTIONS, OR QUESTIONS THAT NEED CLARIFICATION, ETC.	Name: Date: Class: Day: Time: **The PROCTRM Study Technique** **Chapter 7**
	I.) Introduction to the PROCTRM Study Technique
	II.) The PROCTRM Study Technique Explained
	III.) Review of the PROCTRM technique
	I.) Introduction to the PROCTRM Study Technique
	A.
	B.
	1.
	2.
	a.
	b.
	II.) The PROCTRM Study Technique Explained
	A.
	1.
	2.
	B.
	III.) Review of the PROCTRM technique
	A.
	B.
	C.

An example of a PROCTRM note template for left-handed persons

ADDITIONAL NOTES, VOCABULARY DEFINITIONS, EXAMPLES, EXPLANATIONS, POSSIBLE EXAM QUESTIONS, OR QUESTIONS THAT NEED CLARIFICATION, ETC.	Name: Date: Class: Day: Time:

An example of a PROCTRM note template for right-handed persons

NAME: CLASS: DATE: DAY: TIME:	**ADDITIONAL NOTES, VOCABULARY DEFINITIONS, EXAMPLES, EXPLANATIONS, POSSIBLE EXAM QUESTIONS, OR QUESTIONS THAT NEED CLARIFICATION, ETC.**

Step 2: READ

Now, read **_actively_** by highlighting (or underlining) the key ideas, and any definitions, for each section. As you read, underline or circle any vocabulary you are not familiar with. Make a list, or create study cards, and learn them.

This is a very important step. Many people read passively which means that they have no idea where they are going with the reading, and they don't know what to look for along the way.

If you think back to the analogy of the cross-country trip, you will realize that most people want to see points of interest as they travel. A person might map out the route and several sites they would like to visit along the way.

In reading, we should also decide which sites along the way we might want to take notice of. The best way to do that is to highlight as we read.

By highlighting the text as we read, we as in effect putting those words and ideas in neon lights. We are saying, "This is important for me to know and remember."

Now you might be wondering just what to highlight. In the beginning, practice by highlighting what you consider to be important in various magazine articles, novels, and other works that you might read strictly for your own enjoyment. That is called **_Subjective_** highlighting – it depends on the perception, likes and dislikes of the person doing the highlighting. The second type of highlighting is called **_Objective_** highlighting where nearly all persons reading the text would agree on the main points to be highlighted.

We will discuss both of these types of highlighting again as you progress through the text. Also, your instructor will guide you in objective highlighting for the next few chapters. After that point you will have learned the skills necessary to begin objective highlighting on your own.

Step 3: OUTLINE

Once you have actively read and highlighted your chapter, you will be able to create a set of study notes.

Students sometimes are reluctant to create study notes because they see it as more work to do rather than looking at the benefits of creating notes.

Notes benefit us in several ways. Notes help us to organize the information, which is spread over several textbook pages, into a more condensed form. This more condensed form is easier to understand, we can see how the various topics and points relate to one another, and the more organized information is easier for your mind to accept, learn, retain, and recall when needed.

You will become better at creating notes, the more that you practice doing notes. Here's how to start to create a set of good notes:

When creating an outline, you will use your PROCTRM notepaper, beginning with Roman numeral I (from your list created in step 1, and from the highlights for each section) you will fill in the main ideas, and major and minor supporting details section by section (main ideas plus major and minor details were covered in chapter five).

You will do this for all sections listed in your step 1 for each new chapter.

An example of an outline:

I. Topic or Sub-Topic (within a chapter)
    A. Main Idea
        1. Major Supporting Detail
        2. Major Supporting Detail
            a. minor supporting detail
            b. minor supporting detail
                i. additional refining supporting detail
                ii. additional refining supporting detail
    B. Main Idea
        1. Major Supporting Detail
        2. Major Supporting Detail
            a. minor supporting detail
            b. minor supporting detail
                i. additional refining supporting detail
                ii. additional refining supporting detail

Notice that most outlines will contain several levels as shown above. Each level will refine the information or knowledge in more detail. Outlines start with the most general information and each descending level becomes more specific.

Step 4: CRITICAL THINKING

Now you must think critically about what you have outlined. In the small (Left or Right) column (on your PROCTRM note paper), put any questions that need clarification, any insights that you may have gained, and possible exam questions that you anticipate.

It is extremely important to be certain that your notes are complete, and that they make sense – otherwise you may have only performed a lot of copying of information.

Doing some "Critical Thinking" will prepare you to be able to ask intelligent questions during class discussions of the material. In addition to that, it will help you to discover any gaps in your note taking, and help you to prepare for quizzes, and exams.

Step 5: REVIEW

Review your notes often. I would suggest 3 to 5 times a week, and 3 or 4 times per day. Do this simply by rereading them each time. By reviewing your notes often, they will be perceived by your brain as important, and will begin to be stored in your long-term memory.

For information to be retained, it must be perceived by our brain as being important. It must transfer from our short-term memory into our long-term memory. To do this it must be brought to the attention of the mind in a repetitive manner – otherwise the brain usually will not recognize its significance and will only retain it for a brief period in the short-term memory. That is why cramming for an exam usually does not work well. The information is not perceived as important, and as soon as we rest, sleep, or engage in some other activity, the brain begins to delete that information to make room for new, or more important, information.

To illustrate this point, let's compare our mind's makeup to that of a computer. The mind has a short-term memory; the computer has a floppy drive. Both are limited in their capacity to store information and are easily filled. They must be erased (at least in part) to make room for new information.

The mind and computer also have a larger area of storage - with the mind, it is called long-term memory, and with the computer it is called the hard drive. Both of these can accept and store almost limitless information.

To transfer information onto the hard drive, we only need to perform a series of mouse clicks and the information is transferred. To transfer the information   from our short-term memory to our long-term memory, repetition is needed over a period of time. That period of time will vary with each individual, and you will have to determine what works best for you.

Step 6: MEMORIZE

If you have followed steps one through five, then memorizing your notes will be easier than ever before. Much of the information will already be stored in your long-term memory. Now simply check to see what you already know, and then commit the rest to memory.

It's So Easy!

1. Remember this: you probably can't increase your IQ; but you can increase your GPA (grade point average)!!!
2. All you need to do is *use* PROCTRM.
3. Begin to study more ***efficiently*** and higher grades will be your first reward.

Some of the other rewards that will usually come when you have refined your study skills are: a better paying career, more advancement in your career, a newer and better running automobile, a nicer neighborhood to live in, a nicer home or apartment, money for vacations, a happier life, and so much more. What can you add to this list that I haven't mentioned? Take a few minutes and write down some more benefits that might be gained from being able to study better:

_____
_____
_____
_____
_____
_____
_____
_____

III Review of the PROCTRM technique:

There are *six* easy steps to the PROCTRM technique:

1. Preview
2. Read
3. Outline
4. Critical Thinking
5. Review
6. Memorize

It would be a good idea to go back and reread each step now. You will now be able to apply this technique to the remaining chapters in this textbook as well as textbooks for other courses.

As you proceed through each chapter in this text, you will sharpen the skills necessary to become a better reader and you will become more proficient at note taking.

Remember that there are two kinds of highlighting – subjective highlighting and objective highlighting. Practicing both forms will make you a better reader, and you will be able to retain more of what you read through using these processes.

I. From the list of suggested Internet assignments, in the Appendix section of this book, your instructor may assign a topic to research. Actively read the selection, subjectively highlighting as you read. When you finish, reread only the highlighted sections. You should then be able to recall most of the information contained in the article. From just your highlights, retell the story to a friend.

Write that topic here:

_____

Due Date: _____

Additional Instructions or Notes:

_____
_____
_____
_____
_____
_____
_____
_____
_____
_____

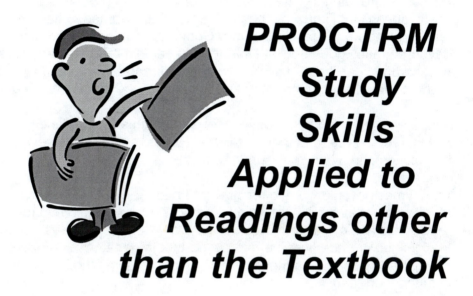

Chapter Eight

PROCTRM Study Skills Applied to Readings other than the Textbook

Introduction

The PROCTRM study method may be modified to fit a variety of reading situations. Some of those applications may include reading newspapers, magazines, short stories, novels or searching the Internet.

In every reading situation, you need to be ready to adapt the technique to fit your needs. The rest of this chapter will give you some valuable insights into adapting your reading, but you may even come up with some creative ideas of your own. Don't be afraid to try new ways of doing things.

PROCTRM Applied to Reading Newspapers & Magazines

I became a reading teacher because I enjoy reading. Sounds pretty basic, doesn't it? I knew by the third grade that I wanted to become a teacher. Knowledge fascinated me. Good books intrigued me, and I devoured many good books. I spent one year just reading every joke book in our local library. I spent two years, during seventh and eighth grade, reading every biography and autobiography that I could find.

My parents received home delivery of a morning and an evening newspaper, so I read both. Later in life, I would subscribe to several magazines and a daily newspaper as well.

Sometimes, I would want to recall what I had read only to find that my recall was not as precise as I would have liked, and I'd have to reread the articles again. To overcome that lack of ("perfect") recall, I began to highlight, or underline, the most important information as I read. By doing that, I was able to trigger my mind into recalling the information in much more detail.

You probably are asking something like, "How did you know what to highlight"? The answer is that at first I didn't know what to highlight, but as I continued to do it, I became sharper at highlighting the really important information. My mind became more selective and tuned into what was really important.

Newspapers are a little bit more difficult to work with because the highlighter will get full of newspaper ink and malfunction. My technique with newspapers was to underline the important information.

Underlining and highlighting in these enjoyable, less threatening, mediums will also sharpen you ability to highlight text in a textbook in a more precise manner.

II. *PROCTRM and the Internet*

The Internet is a great source of valuable information as well as a dumping ground for a lot of kooky ideas. I like to tell my students that just because someone gets published; it does not mean that they know what they are talking about. Jason Blair, who worked for the New York Times is a good example. Much of his material was stolen, or made up, yet his articles were printed at the Times and sent to many other newspaper outlets across the country where they were also printed in local papers.

(b) Another deceptive news reporter was Stephen Glass. In an interview, he admitted that he would start an article with the truth but it would slowly be mixed with false information until by the end of his article it had degenerated into nothing but lies.

Both of these individuals worked for what is termed the "Main Stream Press." If such deception could exist there, we must be even more alert to problems that could evolve on the Internet.

(1) The Internet is open to anyone, to write just about anything, and have it spread around the world with incredible speed before it can be verified. Because of that fact, we must be very careful in what we accept as true. On the upbeat side, the Internet is a great invention for the very fact that nearly everyone can be heard and nearly every point of view can be expressed. It may very well be the freest marketplace for ideas that has ever existed. I hope it remains that way.

(c) Like printed material, we have a responsibility to evaluate the ideas and statement s made over the Internet. One good method for doing that is through a copy and paste technique that I have developed and taught to my students for several years.

The Copy and Paste technique is simple. First, find a web site that you want to copy information from. Next, using your mouse, click and drag over the text that you want to copy. Then, click on the copy symbol at the top of your computer screen (or the word Copy under

75

Edit from the pull down menu). Now, open Microsoft Word or another word processing program, place your curser on the page and click on Paste. Your article will appear and you may print it, highlight it in Word or on the printed sheet, save it to a disk, and increase or decrease the font.

There are also **Download Templates** available on the disk that came with this book. You can open those templates in MS Word and paste your information into them. Then you also have a sidebar for adding your comments about what you are reading. Adding commentary like that is another good technique that will help you to refine your reading skills. It is like going from a monologue, where the printed word speaks to you, to a dialogue, where you also speak back to that printed word.

(2) If you read without responding, you are more likely to be overly influenced by someone's ideas - perhaps even to the point of being "brainwashed." A good dialogue is important. It's okay to write in the side margin why you think the author is wrong. It's also okay to write that the author is right on target in their assessment - of whatever it is that you are reading.

IV PROCTRM Applied to Short Stories & Novels

My friend Elizabeth was an even more avid consumer of reading materials than I. Often I would not have the time to read everything that I wanted to read. Elizabeth, however, often picked books and magazines from my bookshelves and would devour them in record time. Then, she would relate in fine detail every aspect of the story to anyone who would listen. Often I didn't need to read the books after listening to her retelling of what she had read.

Elizabeth possessed a gift that some persons have, but most do not. She had a near photographic recall of whatever she read. I did not possess such a fine gift, and most persons do not possess that ability.

For the rest of us there is the highlighter! Again, highlighting, or underlining, the material can help us to recall it.

(A) When reading novels or short stories, I always highlight the text.① Afterward I would use that highlighting to jog my memory into recalling all of the information. Without highlighting, I found myself lost as to where to begin.

(B) When I was a student, I would also reread my highlights before each class.② I usually scored high on pop quizzes because of that quick review.

(C) In conclusion, as with everything else that we have discussed in this chapter, it is always wise to write commentary in the pages of your book. Carry on a dialogue – don't let it be a monologue! Be involved in the reading process.④ Be an active, not a passive reader.

I.   Using magazines, newspapers, or the Internet, find an article that interests you. Read that article, *highlighting* as you read, and then fill in the information below. Be ready to defend and explain your answers.

    1. What is the topic or title of the article? _____

    2. What are some of the points being expressed in the article?

    _____

    _____

    _____

    _____

    _____

    3. What are some of the details, which the author gives, that support these points?

    _____

    _____

    _____

II.   From the list of suggested Internet assignments, in the Appendix section of this book, your instructor may assign a topic to research.

    Write that topic here:

    _____

    Due Date: _____

    Additional Instructions or Notes:

    _____

    _____

    _____

    _____

    _____

    _____

Chapter Nine

Transitions& Patterns of Organization

I) *Introduction to Transitions*

(A) Transitions are words, or phrases that help to connect thoughts in a person's writing.(1) They are like signs that guide us through a sentence, paragraph, essay, or longer work.(2) They also serve to connect one thought, or series of thoughts, to other ideas as the writing is developed.(3) In this sense, we might think of them as bridges that connect ideas. And, as readers, we need to be aware of these connections.

(4) Through an awareness of these transitions we will be able to better understand the flow of the writer's ideas,(5) better able to identify the supporting details, and(6) better able to highlight the text in order to create outlines that will help us to make sense of, and master, the material.

(B) Some of the more common types of transitions include:(1) addition transitions,(2) time order transitions,(3) example transitions,(4) cause/effect transitions, and(5) comparison and/or contrast transitions.(C) For the next few weeks, it would be wise to underline or circle transitions as you encounter them in print.(4) By doing that, your eyes will become accustomed to noticing these very important transitions, and you will sharpen your skill of handling transitions.

79

I. *Addition Transitions (also called Listing Transitions)*

(A) Addition transitions are easy to understand - they indicate that another point is being *added* to whatever points have already been presented.

Some common addition transitions are:

First or first of all	second / secondly	in conclusion	furthermore
next	third / thirdly	moreover	last (of all)
in addition	finally	another	for one thing

II. *Time Order Transitions*

Time Order transitions are very easy to understand, while also being extremely useful. Time order transitions show us the order in which something happened, or should happen. They guide us in a definite sequence of events (past, present, future) and are often referred to as chronological order. Chrono means time in the Greek language, and logical means that it makes sense. Besides the transitions, time may be indicated by hours, minutes, days, months, years, centuries, and so forth. So we can see that chronological order, or time order, helps us to make sense out of something in a most effective way.

Some common time order transitions:

first	before	later	previously
next	during	now	finally
after	as	when	by
then	while	eventually	after
To begin …	initially	at first	in conclusion

(C) Some authors present their information in the order in which it occurred, others present it using such techniques as flashback – where the events have a time order sequence, but the author has **not** presented them in that sequence. In either case time order does exist and time order transitions are usually used. Our task is to put them in

80

the proper sequence. (3) By noticing the time order transitions we can organize the material into the most logical sequence – even if it was not presented in a straightforward manner.

(4) A time line can also be a very helpful tool which will assist us greatly in mapping out a time order sequence. Simply put, a timeline can be either a vertical, or horizontal line, separated by intersecting lines that indicate at what point an event occurred, or should occur, in relationship to other related events.

(IV) Transitions that Show Examples

(A) Transitions that indicate an example, or examples, are being used will help us to notice supporting details that serve to give legitimacy to the writer's main point, or points, within a piece of writing. Once we take note of these transitions, we can study the examples given to see if they really do support and clarify the author's main point.

Some common example transitions are:

for example	such as	once
for instance	to illustrate	including
another example	an illustration	

(V) Transitions that Show Comparison and/or Contrast

(A) When an author wishes to show us the *similarities* between two things, he/she may use comparison transitions.

Some common comparison transitions are:

like	similar to	resemble
as	in like manner	resembling
just like	in comparison	similarly
alike	just as	in the same way

We can use our awareness of comparison transitions to help us in our mastery of the material that we are studying. To accomplish that goal, we simply need to draw two lines, one horizontal, and one vertical, as illustrated on the next page:

A Comparison chart

	Item A	Item B
	1.	1.
	2.	2.
	3.	3.
	4.	4.
	etc…	etc…

Now, we can *list* the items being *compared* in the selection that we have read and highlighted. In this condensed format, the points compared will be easily received into, remembered by, and retrieved from the brain.

VI Transitions that Show Contrast

Contrast transitions are very important to take notice of. If a reader fails to spot a contrast transition, the whole meaning, and understanding of the piece of writing, is often misunderstood.

Contrast transitions show the *differences* between things being presented in a given piece of writing.

Some common **Contrast** words are:

but	on the contrary	in contrast
yet	in spite of	nevertheless
on the other hand	although	however
conversely	contrary to	despite

We can use our awareness of contrast transitions to help us in our mastery of the material that we are studying. To accomplish that goal, we simply need to draw two lines, one horizontal, and one vertical, as illustrated below:

A Contrast chart

Item A	Item B
1.	1.
2.	2.
3.	3.
4.	4.
etc…	etc…

Now, we can *list* the items being *contrasted* in the selection that we have read and highlighted. In this condensed format, the points contrasted will be easily received into, remembered by, and retrieved from the brain.

VII Comparison and Contrast Transitions Used Together

(A) Often authors will use both comparison and contrast transitions in one piece of writing. When they do that, they want to convey to their readers, the similarities and differences inherent in the information that they are presenting.

From the example charts above, we can see the usefulness of creating charts to assist us in understanding comparisons or contrasts that we might encounter in our readings. In a similar manner, we can construct a chart to show both comparisons and contrasts of information when it is being presented together.

We can use our awareness of comparison/contrast transitions to help us in our mastery of the material that we are studying. To accomplish that goal, we simply need to draw two lines, one horizontal, and one vertical, as illustrated below:

A Comparison/Contrast chart

Item A	Item B
1.	1.
2.	2.
3.	3.
4.	4.
etc…	etc…

(B) Now, we can **list** the items being **compared and/or contrasted** in the selection that we have read and highlighted. In this condensed format, the points compared or contrasted will be easily received into, remembered by, and retrieved from the brain.

VII. Transitions that Show a Cause/Effect Relationship

(A) **Cause and Effect** transitions show us what has happened, why it has happened, and the end results of that occurrence. (1) The cause(s) are the starting point(s), (2) and the effect(s) are the ending point(s). (a) A writer may present one cause, or many causes. Likewise, a writer may present one effect, or several effects.

Some common Cause/Effect transitions are:

because	as a result	because
then	results in	because of
the effect	cause	a reason
an effect	causes	an explanation
one consequence is	effect	so
consequently	effects	led to
as a consequence	if … then	accordingly
since	therefore	leads to

We can use our awareness of cause/effect transitions to help us in our mastery of the material that we are studying. To accomplish that goal, we simply need to draw two lines, one horizontal, and one vertical, as illustrated below:

A Cause/Effect Chart

Cause(s)	Effect(s)
1.	1.
2.	2.
3.	3.
4.	4.
etc…	etc…

(B) Now, we can *list* the cause(s) and effect(s) in the selection that we have read and highlighted. In this condensed format, the *related points* will be easily received into, remembered by, and retrieved from the brain.

IX) *A Paragraph's Topic Sentence*

(A) A paragraph's topic sentence will often provide us with a good indication of the types of transitions to look for. This will also help us to see the patterns of organization often indicated by those transitions. The various patterns of organization will be discussed next.

Introduction to Patterns of Organization

Once you are able to see these patterns, you will be even more effective in understanding information that is presented to you on the printed page. These patterns will show the **_relationships_** between the ideas that support the main idea in paragraphs, or that support the main idea(s) in longer works such as essays, textbook chapters, newspaper or magazine articles, etc.

The Addition Pattern (or the List of Items Pattern) of Organization

The **Addition Pattern**, also called the **List of Items Pattern** uses addition transitions to accomplish its goal of showing the reader that additional items are being presented - in whatever order the author wishes to present them in.

This pattern shows the reader that points are being presented that give additional clarification, validity, explanation, or support for the main idea. They do not have to be presented in any particular order – they are added as the author decides to present them. Rearranging the order would not affect the meaning of the material presented, nor would it affect the reader's understanding of that material. Points are simply **_added_** as one might add items to a grocery list – with no particular order needed.

The Time Order Pattern of Organization

The **_Time Order_** pattern is just as its name suggests, a pattern based on a specific sequence of events, or processes. The items discussed in this pattern follow a specific pattern, and changing that pattern would seriously affect the meaning, and understanding of that piece of writing.

Although the events may not always be presented in perfect time order, the reader must be able to discover that time order sequence, and reconstruct in his/her mind. A useful tool in accomplishing that goal is to create a timeline.

By creating a timeline, the reader can reconstruct the series of events in the order that they occurred, or should occur.

Many areas of study lend themselves well to the time order pattern and we should be aware of this pattern when it is used. History certainly utilizes this pattern, as do the Sciences when describing events and processes. It is extremely important to follow the proper sequences when doing lab experiments, administering medicine to a patient, drawing blood samples, etc.

Even areas of study as diverse as Automotive, Computer Technology, Computer Graphics, Nursing, Mathematics, and Art to name just a few disciplines utilize the Time Order Pattern.

Example Patterns of Organization

Example patterns provide the reader with clearly presented examples that help in the understanding of the main idea. Example patterns may either provide examples that clarify, or expand, on information already presented - or they may be presented to clarify the definition of a word, or term, that has been presented.

These example patterns are easily recognized if we simply watch for transitions indicating that an example, or illustration, is to follow.

When we notice that an example has been provided, it would be wise to mark the page next to that example with an Ex. In this way, you are able to either return to review these examples, without having to search extensively for them, or you are able to notice them more easily when constructing your PROCTRM notes. These examples, or their page locations, can then be easily noted in the small column on your PROCTRM notepaper for later reference if needed.

The Comparison/Contrast Pattern of Organization

The Comparison and/or Contrast patterns show us how material presented is like other material, or how the material is different from other material presented. As has already been stated in chapter five, these patterns are extremely important to notice if a reader is to derive the correct information from the selection being read. Naturally these patterns will become evident to the reader by the reader noticing the Comparison and/or Contrast transitions used.

The Cause/Effect Pattern of Organization

Writers who use the Cause/Effect pattern want to convey to the reader, the causes and effects related to the information that they are presenting. They wish to present information relating to what happened, the reasons why something happened, and the effects of that occurrence. This pattern is useful in presenting events and processes, and you will notice its use in areas of study such as History and the Sciences, as well as in other disciplines.

Mixed Patterns of Organization

Sometimes only one pattern is used in a particular piece of writing, but often more than one pattern is used to convey the writer's knowledge to the reader. When that occurs, there will be a predominant pattern and subordinate pattern, or patterns, presented. The expert reader will utilize the knowledge of these patterns in highlighting, creating notes, and the ultimate mastery of the material.

Topic Sentences and Patterns of Organization

The topic sentence can often indicate the major pattern of organization that will be used in a paragraph or longer piece of writing. By identifying, and noting, the topic sentence (main idea), the astute reader will know the pre-dominant pattern to look for, as well as the transition types that may be used.

A Final Note

All well written works have patterns of organization waiting to be discovered, but transitions, as useful as they are, are not always used by every writer. We must be aware of, and looking for, *the relationships* between ideas, as well as paying attention to the transitions when they are used.

I. *Underline* the transitions used in the following paragraphs and then *write* the type of transitions, and the main pattern of organization, on the lines following each selection.

1. September 11th, 2001 brought profound change to America. As the first plane crashed into the World Trade Center tower, it was uncertain what was happening. After the second plane crashed into the second tower, we knew we were under attack. Now several months later, we are able to understand much more clearly the events of that tragic day.

Type of transitions used: _____
Main Pattern of organization: _____

2. Newspapers are a great source of information concerning current events. First of all, we can read of the national and international news. Next, we can learn about the local happenings. Also, we can learn about sports and sport stars. In addition to all of that, we can view the latest fashions, learn about Hollywood stars, check Real Estate prices, study the Stock Market, and so much more.

Type of transitions used: _____
Main Pattern of organization: _____

3. How can a person plan well for the future? One main way would be to pay attention to whatever is happening in the present. If we are in school, our grades and the knowledge that we gain will influence our future. Another area to pay attention to is the people that we associate with. They will influence decisions today that will affect our future. A third aspect of our life that we must look at is to assess those close relationships that we now have. Is this the person (or persons) that I want to be with in the future?

Type of transitions used: _____

Main Pattern of organization: _____

4. When I went to buy my new car, I studied two cars closely. The first was a Pontiac Firebird. It was sleek and beautiful, red in color, and fast. It had a nice sound as it worked its way through the curves.

    The second car that I drove was a Mustang. It had many of the same characteristics as the Firebird but handled the curves better with less noticeable weight in the front end.

    As a result of studying and driving both cars, I decided on the Mustang.

Type of transitions used: _____

Main Pattern of organization: _____

5. A friend recently told me that he and his wife were waiting to have children until they could afford them. It started me thinking about my own life and how each of my three children had influenced my income. Shortly after the first child was born, I landed a new job and my income increased by fifty percent. The second child came along several years later, and again, shortly after that blessed event, my income doubled. Two years passed and a third child was born, my income again doubled. Now I wonder – was it all coincidental, or is there a connection between having children and your income? Perhaps we can't afford children until after we have them?

Type of transitions used: _____

Main Pattern of organization: _____

6. Did you know that the advice to drink eight glasses of water a day may not be good advice after all? In a recent report, appearing in the August 2002 issue of the *American Journal of Physiology,* Dr. Heinz Valtin studies the confusion and draws certain conclusions. He believes that eating a healthy diet supplies much of the water that we need. Fruits, vegetables, and even meat supply our body with water.) Also, beverages thought to dehydrate the body, such as coffee and tea, actually help to nourish it with water. And a third point he made was that while people with kidney stones require more water than most people, ordinary healthy individuals can drink much less than eight glasses of water a day. In conclusion he says, "Obey your thirst."

Type of transitions used: _____
Main Pattern of organization: _____

7. The great Chicago fire was said to have been started by a cow kicking over a lantern. It began on October 8, 1871, consumed three and a half square miles of the city's buildings while burning for three days. Also, it took two hundred and fifty lives. In addition, property losses were estimated at $200,000,000. Finally, the citizens knew they had to rebuild, and they rebuilt in a finer and grander manner so that the new Chicago was better than the original.

Type of transitions used: _____
Main Pattern of organization: _____

II. Using magazines, newspapers, or the Internet, find an article that interests you. Read that article, *__highlighting all transitions as you read__*, and then fill in the information below. Be ready to defend and explain your answers.

What is the topic or title of the article? _____

    1. What are some of the points being expressed in the article?

       _____

       _____

    2. What are some of the details, which the author gives, that support these points?

       _____

       _____

       _____

       _____

    3. What are six of the transitions used in the reading?

       _____

       _____

       _____

       _____

    4. How did these transitions contribute to your understanding of the reading?

       _____

       _____

       _____

       _____

    5. What is the main pattern of organization used in the article?

       _____

       _____

       _____

       _____

6. What other patterns of organization were used in the selection?

_____

_____

_____

_____

III. From the list of suggested Internet assignments, in the Appendix section of this book, your instructor may assign a topic to research.

Write that topic here:

_____

Due Date: _____

Additional Instructions or Notes:

_____

_____

_____

_____

_____

_____

_____

_____

_____

_____

_____

_____

_____

_____

_____

_____

_____

_____

Chapter Ten

Purpose & Tone

Introduction to Purpose and Tone

In the preceding chapters, we have studied the structure of writing as it relates to refining our reading skills. In this chapter, we will discuss why people write and the various moods, or attitudes, which writers convey.

Purpose

The **Purpose** is the reason why a writer writes something. Have you ever wondered what compelled a particular person to write whatever it is that they wrote? There is always a reason behind the writing. We must remember that all writers are people similar to ourselves, and something has moved them to share a part of their life, their experiences, their thoughts, their imagination, their hope, dreams, despair, etc with the rest of us.

Usually when we study **Purpose**, we tend to focus on three main reasons for a writer sitting down to write. Those three main reasons are:

1. To inform – the writer with this purpose wants to provide information. They want to teach or explain something to us. It could be historical, scientific, political, religious, how to do something, a look at another country, a study of another culture, and so forth. They will try to remain as objective (giving the information without personal bias) as possible.

2. To Persuade – The writer wants to convince us to agree with him/her on a particular subject.
a) It could include any of the items mentioned in our discussion of "To Inform", but in persuasive writing, the author has a particular point of view, or leaning, or bias, or prejudice that can usually be spotted by a sharp reader. They may provide us with facts, but their main objective is to convince us to believe as they do.

3. To entertain – This writer wishes to amuse us, to make us laugh, to make us feel good about ourselves, and the information presented to us.

These are the three main reasons why people write, but writing is not always so clear cut. A writer may use one of these techniques as the predominant mode of expression, but may also mix in either one, or both, of the other reasons for writing as well.

For example, comedians such as Jay Leno or David Letterman may use humor in their act, or writing, yet at the same time influence the political opinions of millions of viewers. Also, a History, or Science textbook writer may include, or leave out, items and information, according to their own personal views on a particular topic.

We must be ever alert to the **purpose** behind the writer sitting down to write in the first place. Some have written works, such as the "Declaration of Independence", that have inspired and uplifted generations, while others have written works, such as "The Prince" by Niccolo Machiavelli, that were designed to deceive and control their populations. Recognizing the purpose is an important step in analyzing anything that we read. If we don't know why a particular piece was written, including some humorous pieces, then we may be led astray.

Tone

A writer's **Tone** projects their feeling towards the subject matter. Another way of thinking about **Tone** is to think of the word **Attitude**. We should ask ourselves what attitude does this writer project. Are they upset, joyful, scholarly, witty, sorrowful, objective, bitter, or a combination of any of these?

There are many feelings, or attitudes, that can be expressed. The list is almost endless, as is the list of human emotions. In the box that follows, are words that describe common tones (you may add a few of your own to the list as well). Most of these words will be familiar to you, but space is provided for you to write in explanations when necessary. The more difficult tones are defined for you. Remember that some tones have similar meanings and may be able to be used interchangeably. The box on the next page will help you to become familiar with many of the common tones that writers use. Remember there also are many more tones that are not included in the list.

Here are some examples of common tones:
(It would be wise to highlight the ones that you are not familiar with and then learn them.)

Tone examples:	Definitions of various tones:
1. angry	Mad
2. forgiving	Not holding a grudge
3. cheerful	Happy
4. caring	Loving and concerned
5. sympathetic	Sharing similar feelings
6. encouraging	Giving hope
7. conceited	Thinking too much of oneself
8. critical	Being too harsh toward others
9. excited	agitated
10. insulting	Saying unkind things
11. sarcastic	Saying things in a biting manner
12. worried	Troubled
13. arrogant	Feeling puffed up, or overly important
14. bitter	Strong feeling of dislike or hatred
15. indignant	Highly insulted
16. upset	Mad, angry
17. concerned	Thoughtful
18. objective	Seeing things as they are
19. subjective	Seeing things through bias, or prejudice
20. pessimistic	Stating that the worst will probably happen
21. optimistic	Stating that things will work out for the best
22. sadness	Not happy
23. sentimental	Having fond memories and a pleasant attitude
24. haughty	A superior attitude
25. nostalgic	Having good memories of the past
26. compassionate	Feeling for others
27. hypocritical	A false manner
28. straightforward	To the point; it is as it is presented
29. deceptive	A false manner
30. tolerant	Able to get along well with others
31. mocking	Making fun of others
32. witty	Funny
33. scholarly	Well written, researched, presented objectively
34. remorseful	Full of regret
35. revengeful	Full of revenge

You may want to add some other tones not covered in the box above.

Tone examples: Definitions of various tones:

Tone examples	Definitions of various tones
1.	
2.	
3.	
4.	
5.	
6.	
7.	
8.	
9.	
10.	

Ironic Tone (or Irony)

An ironic tone is when a writer, or speaker, says one thing but means the opposite of what has been said.

Irony can also refer to situations where the opposite of what we expect to happen, happens.

We must be able to identify an ironic tone when it is used, or we may misunderstand the communication and intentions of the person using that tone. a) Recognizing an ironic tone often draws upon our background knowledge, cultural knowledge, and daily interactions with others. It relies on our ability to infer (figure out) the correct meaning.

I. Read the following sentences carefully, and then write P for persuade, I for inform, or E for entertain.

____ 1. Mama Leone's Spaghetti sauce is the taste of fine Italian cooking.

____ 2. Never turn on a light switch when an odor of leaking gas is present, or you may cause an explosion.

____ 3. "I'd love to help you out; which way did you come in"?

____ 4. Toyota was rated as number one in customer satisfaction for a second year in a row.

____ 5. Some people joke that all lawyers are worse than sharks, but I have found that a good lawyer can protect you from swindlers.

____ 6. Vail Colorado offers some of the very best skiing!

____ 7. Politicians should receive the same percentage of pay increase as the average working person.

____ 8. Domino's pizzas are one of my favorite foods.

____ 9. Very few Americans know what the Constitution says.

____ 10. Voters should vote for the person with the most qualified person, not the best looking.

II. Using magazines, newspapers, or the Internet, find an article that interests you. Read that article, *__highlight words that would indicate purpose or tone,__* and then fill in the information below. Be ready to defend and explain your answers.

1. What is the topic?

_____

_____

2. What are some of the points presented in the story?

_____

_____

_____

3. What are some of the details, which the author gives, that support these points?

_____

_____

_____

_____

4. How would you describe the tone of the story?

_____

_____

_____

_____

5. Why do you think this person wrote this piece?

_____

_____

_____

_____

6. What are six of the transitions used in the reading?

_____

_____

_____

_____

7. How did these transitions contribute to your understanding of the reading?

_____

_____

_____

8. What is the main pattern of organization?

_____

_____

_____

9. Were any other patterns used in the reading? If so, what are they?

_____

_____

_____

III. From the list of suggested Internet assignments, in the Appendix section of this book, your instructor may assign a topic to research.

Write that topic here:

_____

Due Date: _____

Additional Instructions or Notes:

_____

_____

_____

_____

_____

_____

_____

_____

_____

_____

_____

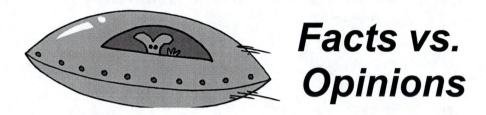

Chapter Eleven

Facts vs. Opinions

Introduction to Facts vs. Opinions

Most of what we read, and hear, we assume to be factual, but actually it usually is someone's opinion. B) People love to give their opinions on any number of topics, and often portray themselves as experts on the subject matter at hand, but that confident, assuring attitude can lead us astray if we are not well versed in the differences between Facts and Opinions.

This chapter, on the surface, may look simplistic, but a thorough study of Facts vs. Opinions will probably convince you otherwise.

Facts

Just what are Facts? We know that, for centuries, most people believed that the earth was flat. Sailors were afraid to sail too far, for fear of falling off the edge of the world. People were put to death for believing, or teaching that the earth might be round. Today, we know without a doubt, that the earth is round and feel sorry for those who lost their lives for their beliefs that contradicted the "facts" of that time period.

There are Two Types of Facts: Assumed Facts and Proven Facts

Assumed Facts

An **assumed fact** is a fact that we assume to be true because the majority of people believe it, no one has been able to disprove it, and it seems correct.

Proven Facts

A **proven fact** is a fact that has been proven to the extent that there is no room for doubt or controversy. Today, we would all agree that the earth is "round" and we can verify its roundness through photos from satellites in space and many other sources.

Opinions

Most of what we read, hear, and see are opinions being expressed. Almost everyone has an opinion on almost anything, anyone, and any topic. Opinions are not necessarily bad or destructive. Actually opinions make the world an interesting place. But, we must remember that opinions are not facts.

Opinions are the expressions of a person, or group's, perception of this very complex world. Those perceptions may be affected by any number of things such as: environment, religion or lack of religion, political views, gender, sexual orientation, family life or lack of family life, any of life's various experiences – both good or bad, social status, education, language proficiency, cultural background, and so forth. The list is endless, and so are the ways in which people perceive the world, react to it, and form opinions.

Opinions are **subjective** (based on the subject's perceptions) and cannot be proven true or false. We must learn to respect the diverse opinions in our world – even when we disagree.

Opinions usually express a *value* and persons expressing opinions use *value words*. These value words indicate that an opinion is being expressed, and we should be finely tuned to listening for them in conversations, and watching for them in our readings. Value words indicate that a judgment is being made that either favors or demotes something, someone, or some group. Watching for value words is one method that enables us to separate fact from opinion. In the box on the next page are some common value words. You may also want to add some of you own to the list.

105

Examples of Value Words: Common Definitions of those words:

Examples of Value Words:	Common Definitions of those words:
1. best	
2. worst	
3. ugliest	
4. prettiest	
5. most handsome	
6. meanest	
7. tallest	
8. biggest	
9. smallest	
10. most important	
11. I think	
12. I believe	
13. should	
14. ought to	
15. wonderful	

Being Too Inclusive

When a person uses words such as: *all, everyone, all believe, or everyone knows*, or similar expressions, they are usually expressing an opinion. There rarely is 100% agreement on any issue as indicated by these words.

Opinions Presented as Facts

Very often, speakers and writers will present their opinions as if they were facts. As *active readers*, we must be aware of this problem. 2) We should have a keen eye for *value words*, which as we have already noted, express opinions not facts.

We also need to distinguish between assumed facts and proven facts.

Often people will use words, or phrases, like: as a matter of fact, in fact, it's a well known fact, the truth of the matter, clearly, everyone knows, everyone believes, all agree, etc. These words, however, by themselves are not proof of factual information and we must discern whether facts or opinions are actually being expressed and to do that, we must be active and alert when we read.

Using a highlighter can assist you greatly in separating facts from opinions. Look first for the main idea, then value words, and finally look at the supporting details. Do they represent facts or opinions? A fact should be *objective* in nature, and report on observed and verified (or verifiable) reality. An opinion is *subjective,* and is interpreting or evaluating, the subject matter.

Both facts and opinions have their place in the various ways that we communicate but we must be able to distinguish between the two.

The Mixture of Facts and Opinions

Remember, much of what we read, and hear, is a mixture of facts and opinions. Also, many people are skilled at making opinions appear to be facts. While both are important to our everyday communication, we must be able to separate one from the other. This is one very important skill that will separate a *truly educated* person from those who are often naïve, gullible, and manipulated in their everyday life. Being a critical reader is important to functioning well in our fast paced world.

I. Write AF for assumed fact, PF for proven fact, O for opinion, and F+O for a combination of fact and opinion.

_AF_ 1. Students who sit at the front of the class always receive the highest grades.

_O_ 2. Everyone knows Arnold would be a better governor than Gray Davis.

_O_ 3. George W. Bush is a great president!

_PF_ 4. I have measured everyone and Sandra is the tallest person in our class.

_PF_ 5. One of the worst tasting foods, which I have ever attempted to eat, was shark.

_AF_ 6. Most people believe that Betsy Ross sewed the first American flag.

_AF_ 7. Everyone knows that Canada is our Northern neighbor.

_PF_ 8. Copper is a good even heat conductor for pots and pans.

_PF_ 9. Aluminum wiring was found to be dangerous.

_PF/O_ 10. Today's computers are much more advanced than those of fifteen years ago, and clearly Dell computers are the best new computers available.

II. Using magazines, newspapers, or the Internet, find an article that interests you. ***Read that article and highlight the words, or phrases, or sentences, that indicate either a fact being expressed or an opinion being presented.*** **Note** on your article whether it is a fact or opinion being expressed. Finally, fill in the information below. Be ready to defend and explain your answers.

1. What is the topic or title of the article? _____

2. What are some of the points being expressed in the article?
   _____
   _____
   _____

3. What are some of the details, which the author gives, which support these points?
   _____
   _____
   _____

4. How would you describe the tone of the article?
   _____
   _____
   _____

5. Why do you think this person wrote that piece?
   _____
   _____
   _____

6. List three facts that you discovered in the reading selection.
   _____
   _____
   _____

7. List three opinions that you encountered in the reading selection.
   _____
   _____
   _____
   _____

III. From the list of suggested Internet assignments, in the Appendix section of this book, your instructor may assign a topic to research.

Write that topic here:

_____

Due Date: _____

Additional Instructions or Notes:

_____
_____
_____
_____
_____
_____
_____
_____
_____
_____
_____
_____
_____
_____
_____
_____
_____
_____
_____
_____
_____
_____
_____
_____
_____
_____
_____
_____

Chapter Twelve

The Newspaper

An Introduction to the Newspaper

When I was a child, every morning and every afternoon a newspaper would be delivered to our home. We lived in the north-east area of New York State where the four seasons were a definite part of our life. Because of that fact, I have always had a connection in my mind, and senses, between the newspaper and the weather.

 On cold snowy days, I would feel the blast of cold air on my face and the rush of cold air down into my lungs as I hurriedly picked the paper from the ground and rushed back indoors to read it.

When spring arrived, I would smell the flower blossoms and feel relieved that winter was once again behind us for a few months and I would slowly pick up the newspaper, pause for another breath of spring air, and then casually sit to read the paper.

The summer heat would blast at my face and the humidity would drench me with sweat as I once again picked the paper from the ground and returned to the house to read it.

 I would often sit at the kitchen table or on the living room couch and read whatever caught my eye. I would usually read the sports section and comics, and then local and national news.

My dad would usually read the paper as he drank his coffee before rushing off to work and then again after supper. Mom would read the paper after she fed us our breakfast and saw us off to school or after she tucked us into bed after a long day of raising eight children.

So reading the newspaper was a normal daily activity at our house, but that is not the case today in most homes. Today people seem more rushed than ever before and many often gather their news from the Internet or the television news broadcasts as they hurry through each day.

The news that most of us gather in that manner is very condensed and often biased. The newspaper on the other hand can provide us with more in-depth coverage of the news that may affect our lives both on a local and national level. It also allows us a chance to sit and reflect upon what we have just read and gives us the opportunity to read it again if we so desire.

Why do People Either Read or Not Read the Newspaper?

Take a few minutes to write why you think people either read or do not read the newspaper.

Why people <u>do</u> read the newspaper:

1. _____
2. _____
3. _____
4. _____
5. _____
6. _____
7. _____
8. _____
9. _____
10. _____

Why people <u>don't</u> read the newspaper:

1. _____
2. _____
3. _____
4. _____
5. _____
6. _____
7. _____
8. _____
9. _____
10. _____

Now take a few moments to think about why people <u>should</u> read the newspaper:

Why people should read the newspaper:

1. _____
2. _____
3. _____
4. _____
5. _____
6. _____
7. _____
8. _____
9. _____
10. _____

How often do you read a newspaper?

_____
_____
_____
_____
_____

Why Buy a Newspaper? It's More Than Just News!

 Because newspapers cost money, many people are reluctant to buy them. There has to be a value to every item that we purchase or we probably will not want to spend our money on it.

One reason for buying a newspaper would be that you will become a more informed citizen. That will add to your ability to communicate with, and interact with, others. You will have more to talk about and you will be able to base your opinions upon knowledge.

Reading newspapers also helps an individual reinforce and expand upon their vocabulary. As your vocabulary grows, your chances for advancement in most professions also grow, and that usually means an increase in your paycheck.

The Many Parts of the Newspaper

The newspaper is composed of many parts and that may change daily. The sections that are always present are National News, Local News, Sports, and Classified. Other sections that may appear on certain days are Lifestyles, Religion, Travel, Work and Money, Food, Technology, and other special inserts.

 As you read the National news, you'll learn about the national politics and the national leaders of our nation. You'll study events taking place around the nation and around the world and hopefully you'll have a better understanding of the world that we live in.

From the Local section, you will know what is happening in your area. You will learn of local problems, local events, local school activities, good or bad neighborhoods, and the overall pros and cons of living in your area.

The Comic section can provide a quick laugh or uplifting of our mood. It can also be a place where political satire is presented to the reader so it may not always be just about laughs.

 The Sports section can instill pride in us of the achievements of various athletes.

The Food section can add interesting foods to our menu. It can offer us advice on cooking a variety of dishes from many cultures.

The Weather section can inform us of the type of clothing to wear that day, or even that week, and can help us to avoid being surprised by storms.

The Classified Ads section can help us to find automobiles, homes, apartments, furniture, and other items for sale. It can also help us to sell unwanted items in an ad or help us conduct, or find, a yard sale.

The Work and Money section provides us with an insight into the job market both on the local and national levels. It can give us an overall picture of the nation's economy and help us to make wise decisions concerning our money and our credit worthiness.

The Religion section lets us experience different cultures and their belief systems. It gives us a valuable insight into the beliefs and customs of many religions and philosophies that exist in our world and hopefully that will make everyone more accepting of the differences that exist.

The Lifestyles section presents us with a view into modern culture and cultural events. It also discusses health and fitness with articles that address proper eating habits, good exercise habits, and medical treatments if health breaks down.

Advertisements and coupons in the paper give an opportunity to save money. We can become wiser consumers by reading the ads and looking through the fliers that often accompany the paper. By buying food items when they are on sale, you may save a significant amount on your food bill. Cutting out coupons for items that you normally purchase can also contribute to savings at the grocery store.

Recently my family purchased a new dining room table and chair set. We were able to save about $800 off of the normal price because we saw the ad in the newspaper. That purchase alone pays for the paper for several months if not years. Also, during the past few years, I have saved money on electronic purchases, a lawnmower, a refrigerator, a stove, a patio set, and a trailer for my kayaks by knowing where to shop for the best deals according to the newspaper ads. So a newspaper can actually pay for itself, or even save you money, while at the same time providing you with all of the benefits mentioned above and so much more.

Who is Behind Your Newspaper?

I have said many nice things in support of the newspaper but now I will voice some concerns. We don't live in a perfect world and almost everything that exists can have a positive side and a negative side.

When I was taught about the newspaper in school, I was told that all newspapers are unbiased and contain the unadulterated truth. I doubt if that was the case then and I know that is not the case today.

My first wakeup call came when I was in college in the turbulent 1960s. There was a shootout in Chicago between the police and a radical group. The radical group was in a small cabin-like building and one Chicago newspaper account said that the radical group refused to surrender, a shoot out occurred, the building caught fire, and they burned to death.

The newspaper also included a picture of a door that had survived the fire, and it showed bullet holes from the radicals firing out at the police.

The next day, however, the other Chicago newspaper showed the picture of the same door and said that the bullet holes were actually

roofing nails that had been pounded into the door to look like bullet holes.

I don't know what happened that day between the police and the radical group but I do know that my faith in unbiased newspaper reporting was shattered. I learned to examine and question everyone and everything much more closely.

I also learned that people and nations can be influenced, controlled, and manipulated by unscrupulous people who own and control newspapers and other media. So, it is our responsibility to read newspapers, listen to newscasts, read web articles and web news, and read books and magazines with a very questioning mind.

It is sad that news sources cannot be trusted to just report the facts, but the truth is that much manipulation does occur. So, as a result, we have news that is accurate, and we have news that is biased or sometimes even made up. That is the world that we live in. We must decide what sources of information are most reliable and use those sources while steering clear of sources that have a past record of biased reporting.

Connotative Words

Be always on the lookout for connotative words when reading the newspapers or any other written piece. Connotative words are words that are meant to stir our emotions. Newspapers should report the facts and should not be stirring our emotions. You should be able to think about what you have read rather than react to it without much thinking.

Newspapers Share News Stories & Articles

The Associated Press

 The Associated Press (AP) is the oldest and largest cooperative news source in the world today. It was founded in 1848 to provide news to six large New York newspapers but it has grown since then to now serve over 1,700 U.S. newspapers and 5,000 broadcast outlets as well as many newspaper outlets worldwide. It has 242 bureaus worldwide that work to provide the Associated Press with current news from around the world. It is owned by its 1,700 subscribing newspapers in the U.S and they elect a board of directors to oversee its operations.

On any given day, over half of the world's population reads or sees news from the Associated Press. This fact bestows upon the AP the responsibility to ensure that their news reporting is accurate and free of bias. So far, the Associated Press has a good track record when it comes to accurate news reporting, but, as stated above, we must be critical consumers when it comes to the news whether in print, on the Internet, on radio, or on television.

The AP employs many very good and experienced journalists from many parts of the world. Often their news stories would not be available from any other source. Reporters who violate the rules of fairness, balance, and accuracy are usually reprimanded severely, or removed entirely from AP employment, so few violate the standards.

The AP Exchange allows newspaper editors and reporters access to the many stories in the AP data base. These stories are often purchased by the 1,700 newspapers or the 5,000 broadcast outlets and other media outlets in the U.S. as well as other newspaper and media sources worldwide. The AP also provides a data base of photos and video clips that may be used by their subscribing news outlets worldwide.

This works well if the stories are fair, balanced and accurate. It would be terrible however if those standards are ever compromised since the world could then be fed lies on a world wide scale. The consequences could be the rise of dictators on a level such as the world has never before experienced. That is why all of us must remain vigilant when it comes to the truth in news reporting.

Other Ways Newspapers Share Their News

Besides the AP, most newspapers buy from and sell to other newspapers around the world. If a story is accurate, it is an efficient and cost effective way to cover the news. If a story is inaccurate, it is a way for an erroneous story to be spread though many newspapers or other media outlets.

Sometimes a newspaper is owned by a person or group that has a certain political or social agenda that they want to push on society. They can be a dangerous influence on society even to the point of brainwashing the citizens who read their papers. Again as consumers, we must be ever vigilant that this may occur. Powerful people often buy newspapers and other media outlets so that they can influence the thinking and values of the public. A look at several newspapers and several news broadcasts will show you the similarities and differences that exist in the marketplace today. You will have to decide what is accurate, fair, and balanced. The skills in the other chapters of this textbook will help you to do that.

STALIN

Each article in the newspaper will have the original source printed under the author's name. That is a good reference point and it will help you in determining an articles worth. If you know that a certain newspaper usually prints accurate articles then you need to exercise less caution than if the source is one that has been biased in the past.

Some Modern Villains

We have some recent examples of persons manipulating the news media. Jason Blair and Steven Glass are two reporters who mixed truth with lies, facts with opinions, and successfully deceived thousands if not millions of readers.

Jason Blair lied about where he was, what he claimed to see, who he talked to, and many other things. He made up stories about the war in Iraq, the D.C. sniper case and much more.

In the D.C. sniper case he wrote that a confession was about to come from at least one of the men involved in the shootings but the interrogators decided to break for lunch. When they returned from lunch, Blair claimed that the sniper had decided not to confess.

This story was carried nationally and in several newspapers around the world. Of course, the interrogators denied that this scenario ever happened but Jason Blair and most newspapers stood by the story!

To a rational thinking person, the story is ludicrous. No interrogator is going to break for lunch when a confession is forthcoming, yet this was printed and many people believed it.

He had his articles corrected over fifty times yet he was not fired until the outcry from the public became so great that the newspaper and its editors could no longer ignore, or perhaps cover up, his malicious deeds.

Now, we must ask ourselves, "Why did the New York Times put up with his shoddy reporting for so long"?

Jason Blair answered that question in a televised interview by stating that he felt the paper had a social change agenda. They wanted to influence their readers to accept a particular political bias. In his opinion, as long as he was writing articles that fit their agenda (whether true or not), he would not be fired.

That is a serious threat to our freedom. Their "agenda" may even fit my, or your, philosophy of life, but lying to the public, instead of reporting the factual news, should never be accepted. It may very well lead us down the path to tyranny.

Another point worth repeating here is that lies that are printed in one paper are easily bought by other editors and printed elsewhere so the lie or bias may spread very quickly.

For more information on this topic, Jason Blair has written a book entitled *Burning Down My Masters House*.

 Another reporter who lied and manipulated the press was Steven Glass and a movie was made chronicling his story called *Shattered Glass*. He created fake notes, fake faxes, phony websites, fake business cards and more in order to write false articles for newspapers and magazines.

He says that he would sometimes write entire articles that were total lies while at other times he would mix truth with lies in order to deceive his bosses and readers. He was often vicious in his attacks on people. Here again we have another case of a reporter who deceived his audience but he was finally discovered for the manipulator that he was, and then he was fired.

Dan Rather, in a television interview, said, "I think you can be an honest person and lie about any number of things." This statement was made by a man who reported the news for CBS television for about 25 years. It flies in the face of the definition of an honest person. An honest person may lie once in a while but not on a continuous basis. The definition of a dishonest person might be a person who can "… lie about any number of things." We should all be concerned when truth and lies are so easily interchanged in a person's mind!

Let me be very clear that I think that many journalists are very good and very honest, but there are also many who will act like Jason Blair, Steven Glass and Dan Rather if they feel that they can get away with their lies. We must use our reading and thinking skills so that we do not become fooled by the deceivers of the world.

Photo manipulation

As I stated above, photos were manipulated in the 1960s when technology was not as advanced as today. Not only must we question what we read but we must question what we see in photos and motion pictures.

Photos are often cropped and doctored to manipulate us through our eyes. The photos that are printed as well as those that are not printed can greatly influence our thinking on war, politics, people in the news, political leaders, political candidates, and so much more. Again fair reporting is what we should be getting but we often do not receive.

Doctored pictures by a reporter named Adnon Haj were discovered by Reuters news service and were purged from their system but many of the doctored photos had already been published. In one photo, missiles had been copied and pasted to make a military attack look more ominous. In another photo, smoke from dropped bombs had been darkened and then copied and pasted to make an attack look more sinister.

In the late 1990s a movie was made which clearly shows how film may be manipulated. In Wag the Dog a young girl is running across a stage holding a bag of chips. After some studio manipulation, she is digitally made to be carrying a kitten across a burning bridge with the wail of sirens in the background. Supposedly she is now a refugee fleeing for her life. It is a mediocre movie in my opinion but clearly illustrates what can be done with film. In a movie, it is harmless entertainment, in real life, it can produce manipulation of entire populations in the hands of an evil person.

Keeping a Newspaper Portfolio

Despite all of the warning that I have given above, I still believe that a person should buy and read the newspaper, but we have to discern which newspaper will give us accurate reporting and which will not before we spend our money.

A good way to evaluate and enjoy a newspaper is to create a scrapbook, or portfolio, of newspaper articles. Start by reading whatever you find most interesting, then cut it out and start to build your collection. The articles could be pasted onto paper and bound, or slipped into plastic sleeves and kept in a ring binder notebook. Another activity would be to scan them into your computer and save them in a folder on your hard drive.

In closing, I hope that you will weigh the benefits vs. the pitfalls of reading the newspaper. I also hope that you will read carefully and become a concerned and well informed citizen. Remember to underline and annotate your articles to help you in your critique of what you are reading and then question everything and everyone.

Part 2

Reading Selections

Vocabulary Preview: These words may present challenges when reading. Preview them now, and return to them again if you need to.

Challenging words: A common definition:

1.	
2.	
3.	
4.	
5.	
6.	
7.	
8.	
9.	
10.	
11.	
12.	
13.	
14.	
15.	
16.	
17.	
18.	
19.	
20.	
21.	
22.	
23.	
24.	
25.	

Vocabulary Preview: These words may present challenges when reading. Preview them now, and return to them again if you need to.

Challenging words:	A common definition:
1.	
2.	
3.	
4.	
5.	
6.	
7.	
8.	
9.	
10.	
11.	
12.	
13.	
14.	
15.	
16.	
17.	
18.	
19.	
20.	
21.	
22.	
23.	
24.	
25.	

AN ANECDOTE OF DOCTOR FRANKLIN

by Thomas Jefferson

When the Declaration of Independence was under the consideration of Congress, there were two or three unlucky expressions in it which gave offence to some members. The word "Scotch and other foreign auxiliaries" excited the ire of a gentleman or two of that country.

Severe strictures on the conduct of the British King, in negotiating our repeated repeals of the law which permitted the importation of slaves, were disapproved by some Southern gentlemen, whose reflections were not yet matured to the full abhorrence of that traffic. Although the offensive expressions were immediately yielded, these gentlemen continued their depredations on other parts of the instrument.

I was sitting by Dr. Franklin, who perceived that I was not insensible to these mutilations. "I have made it a rule," said he, "whenever in my power, to avoid becoming the draughtsman of papers to be reviewed by a public body. I took my lesson from an incident which I will relate to you.

When I was a journeyman printer, one of my companions, an apprentice hatter, having served out his time, was about to open shop for himself. His first concern was to have a handsome signboard, with a proper inscription.

He composed it in these words, 'John Thompson, Hatter, makes and sells hats for ready money,' with a figure of a hat subjoined; but he thought he would submit it to his friends for their amendments.

The first he showed it to thought the word 'Hatter' tautologous, because followed by the words 'makes hats,' which show he was a hatter.

It was struck out.

The next observed that the word 'makes' might as well be omitted, because his customers would not care who made the hats. If good and to their mind, they would buy, by whomsoever made.

He struck it out.

A third said he thought the words 'for ready money' were useless as it was not the custom of the place to sell on credit. Every one who purchased expected to pay. They were parted with, and the inscription now stood, 'John Thompson sells hats.'

'Sells hats,' says his next friend! Why nobody will expect you to give them away, what then is the use of that word?

It was stricken out, and 'hats' followed it, the rather as there was one painted on the board.

So the inscription was reduced ultimately to 'John Thompson' with the figure of a hat subjoined."

Name: _____

Reading Selection: _____

1. **What is the author's overall main idea, (central point, or thesis)?**
_____
_____

2. **There are two kinds of supporting details--major and minor. Major details are the primary points that support the main idea and minor details expand major details. List <u>three</u> details and explain how they support the author's primary point?**

Details used	Explanation of how they support the thesis
1.	

Details used	Explanation of how they support the thesis
2.	

Details used	Explanation of how they support the thesis
3.	

3. **The five <u>main</u> patterns of organization are the list of items pattern, the time order pattern, the example pattern, the comparison and/or contrast pattern, and the cause/effect pattern. What is the <u>main</u> pattern of organization used in this article? <u>Explain</u> why it is the main pattern. What other patterns are used? Give some examples.**

Main pattern:
_____

Explain how the <u>main pattern</u> was used:
_____
_____

Write five of the transitions that helped indicate the <u>main pattern</u> of this selection:
_____ _____ _____ _____ _____

Other pattern(s) used:

_____

Explain how the additional pattern(s) were used:

_____
_____

What were some of the transitions that helped you to discover the other patterns?

_____ _____ _____ _____ _____

4. List <u>three</u> facts in the article. <u>Explain why</u> each it is a fact.

	Explanation:
A.) fact:	A.)
B.) fact:	B.)
C.) fact:	C.)

5. List <u>three</u> opinions in the article. <u>Explain why</u> each it is an opinion.

	Explanation:
A.) opinion	A.)
B.) opinion:	B.)
C.) opinion:	C.)

6. What is the author's main purpose in writing this article? Is it to inform, persuade, or entertain? <u>Tell me how you arrived at that conclusion.</u>

_____
_____
_____

7. What is the author's main tone? <u>Explain how you arrived at your answer.</u>

_____
_____
_____

Vocabulary Preview: These words may present challenges when reading. Preview them now, and return to them again if you need to.

Challenging words: A common definition:

1.	
2.	
3.	
4.	
5.	
6.	
7.	
8.	
9.	
10.	
11.	
12.	
13.	
14.	
15.	
16.	
17.	
18.	
19.	
20.	
21.	
22.	
23.	
24.	
25.	

Vocabulary Preview: These words may present challenges when reading. Preview them now, and return to them again if you need to.

Challenging words:	A common definition:
1.	
2.	
3.	
4.	
5.	
6.	
7.	
8.	
9.	
10.	
11.	
12.	
13.	
14.	
15.	
16.	
17.	
18.	
19.	
20.	
21.	
22.	
23.	
24.	
25.	

DOWN
THE RABBIT-HOLE

from Alice in Wonderland by Lewis Carroll

Commentary or Analysis:

ALICE was beginning to get very tired of sitting by her sister on the bank and of having nothing to do: once or twice she had peeped into the book her sister was reading, but it had no pictures or conversations in it, "and what is the use of a book," thought Alice, "without pictures or conversations?"

So she was considering, in her own mind (as well as she could, for the hot day made her feel very sleepy and stupid), whether the pleasure of making a daisy-chain would be worth the trouble of getting up and picking the daisies, when suddenly a White Rabbit with pink eyes ran close by her.

There was nothing so very remarkable in that; nor did Alice think it so very much out of the way to hear the Rabbit say to itself "Oh dear! Oh dear! I shall be too late!" (when she thought it over afterwards it occurred to her that she ought to have wondered at this, but at the time it all seemed quite natural); but, when the Rabbit actually took a watch out of its waistcoat-pocket, and looked at it, and then hurried on, Alice started to her feet, for it flashed across her mind that she had never before seen a rabbit with either a waistcoat-pocket, or a watch to take out of it, and burning with curiosity, she ran across the field after it, and was just in time to see it pop down a large rabbit-hole under the a large rabbit-hole under the hedge.

In another moment down went Alice after it, never once considering how in the world she was to get out again.

The rabbit-hole went straight on like a tunnel for some way, and then dipped suddenly down, so suddenly that Alice had not a moment to think about stopping herself

135

before she found herself falling down what seemed to be a very deep well.

Either the well was very deep, or she fell very slowly, for she had plenty of time as she went down to look about her, and to wonder what was going to happen next. First, she tried to look down and make out what she was coming to, but it was too dark to see anything: then she looked at the sides of the well, and noticed that they were filled with cupboards and book-shelves: here and there she saw maps and pictures hung upon pegs. She took down a jar from one of the shelves as she passed: it was labeled "ORANGE MARMALADE" but to her great disappointment it was empty: she did not like to drop the jar, for fear of killing somebody underneath, so managed to put it into one of the cupboards as she fell past it.

"Well!" thought Alice to herself. "After such a fall as this, I shall think nothing of tumbling down-stairs! How brave they'll all think me at home! Why, I wouldn't say anything about it, even if I fell off the top of the house!" (Which was very likely true.)

Down, down, down. Would the fall never come to an end?

"I wonder how many miles I've fallen by this time?" she said aloud. "I must be getting somewhere near the centre of the earth. Let me see: that would be four thousand miles down, I think-" (for, you see, Alice had learnt several things of this sort in her lessons in the school-room, and though this was not a very good opportunity for showing off her knowledge, as there was no one to listen to her, still it was good practice to say it over) "-yes that's about the right distance- but then I wonder what Latitude or Longitude I've got to?" (Alice had not the slightest idea what Latitude was, or Longitude either, but she thought they were nice grand words to say.)

Presently she began again. "I wonder if I shall fall right through the earth! How funny it'll seem to come out among the people that walk with their heads downwards! The antipathies, I think-" (she was rather glad there was no one listening, this time, as it didn't sound at all the right word) "-but I shall have to ask them what the name of the country is, you know. Please, Ma'am, is this New Zealand? Or Australia?" (and she tried to curtsey as she spoke- fancy, curtseying as you're falling through the air! Do you think you could manage it?) "And what an ignorant little girl she'll think me for asking!

No, it'll never do to ask: perhaps I shall see it written up somewhere."

Down, down, down. There was nothing else to do, so Alice soon began talking again. "Dinah'll miss me very much to-night, I should think!" (Dinah was the cat.) "I hope they'll remember her saucer of milk at tea-time. Dinah, my dear! I wish you were down here with me! There are no mice in the air, I'm afraid, but you might catch a bat, and that's very like a mouse, you know. But do cats eat bats, I wonder?" And here Alice began to get rather sleepy, and went on saying to herself, in a dreamy sort of way, "Do cats eat bats? Do cats eat bats?" and sometimes "Do bats eat cats?" for, you see, as she couldn't answer either question, it didn't much matter which way she put it. She felt that she was dozing off, and had just begun to dream that she was walking hand in hand with Dinah, and was saying to her, very earnestly, "Now, Dinah, tell me the truth: did you ever eat a bat?" when suddenly, thump! thump! down she came upon a heap of sticks and dry leaves, and the fall was over.

Alice was not a bit hurt, and she jumped up on to her feet in a moment: she looked up, but it was all dark overhead: before her was another long passage, and the White Rabbit was still in sight, hurrying down it. There was not a moment to be lost: away went Alice like the wind, and was just in time to hear it say, as it turned a corner, "Oh my ears and whiskers, how late it's getting!" She was close behind it when she turned the corner, but the Rabbit was no longer to be seen: she found herself in a long, low hall, which was lit up by a row of lamps hanging from the roof.

There were doors all round the hall, but they were all locked; and when Alice had been all the way down one side and up the other, trying every door, she walked sadly down the middle, wondering how she was ever to get out again.

Suddenly she came upon a little three-legged table, all made of solid glass: there was nothing on it but a tiny golden key, and Alice's first idea was that this might belong to one of the doors of the hall; but, alas! either the locks were too large, or the key was too small, but at any rate it would not open any of them. However, on the second time round, she came upon a low curtain she had not noticed before, and behind it was a little door about fifteen inches high: she tried the little golden key in the lock, and to her great delight it fitted!

Alice opened the door and found that it led into a small passage, not much larger than a rat-hole: she knelt down and looked along the passage into the loveliest garden you ever saw. How she longed to get out of that dark hall, and wander about among those beds of bright flowers and those cool fountains, but she could not even get her head through the doorway; "and even if my head would go through," thought poor Alice, "it would be of very little use without my shoulders. Oh, how I wish I could shut up like a telescope! I think I could, if I only knew how to begin." For, you see, so many out-of-the-way things had happened lately, that Alice had begun to think that very few things indeed were really impossible.

There seemed to be no use in waiting by the little door, so she went back to the table, half hoping she might find another key on it, or at any rate a book of rules for shutting people up like telescopes: this time she found a little bottle on it, ("which certainly was not here before," said Alice), and tied round the neck of the bottle was a paper label, with the words "DRINK ME" beautifully printed on it in large letters.

It was all very well to say "Drink me," but the wise little Alice was not going to do that in a hurry. "No, I'll look first," she said, "and see whether it's marked 'poison' or not"; for she had read several nice little stories about children who had got burnt, and eaten up by wild beasts, and other unpleasant things, all because they would not remember the simple rules their friends had taught them:

138

such as, that a red-hot poker will burn you if you hold it too long; and that, if you cut your finger very deeply with a knife, it usually bleeds; and she had never forgotten that, if you drink much from a bottle marked "poison," it is almost certain to disagree with you, sooner or later.

However, this bottle was not marked "poison," so Alice ventured to taste it, and, finding it very nice (it had, in fact, a sort of mixed flavour of cherry-tart, custard, pine-apple, roast turkey, toffy, and hot buttered toast), she very soon finished it off.

"What a curious feeling!" said Alice. "I must be shutting up like a telescope!"

And so it was indeed: she was now only ten inches high, and her face brightened up at the thought that she was now the right size for going through the little door into that lovely garden. First, however, she waited for a few minutes to see if she was going to shrink any further: she felt a little nervous about this; "for it might end, you know," said Alice to herself, "in my going out altogether, like a candle. I wonder what I should be like then?" And she tried to fancy what the flame of a candle looks like after the candle is blown out, for she could not remember ever having seen such a thing.

After a while, finding that nothing more happened, she decided on going into the garden at once; but, alas for poor Alice! when she got to the door, she found she had forgotten the little golden key, and when she went back to the table for it, she found she could not possibly reach it: she could see it quite plainly through the glass, and she tried her best to climb up one of the legs of the table, but it was too slippery; and when she had tired herself out with trying, the poor little thing sat down and cried.

"Come, there's no use in crying like that!" said Alice to herself rather sharply. "I advise you to leave off this minute!" She generally gave herself very good advice (though she very seldom followed it), and sometimes she scolded herself so severely as to bring tears into her eyes; and once she remembered trying to box her own ears for having cheated herself in a game of croquet she was playing against herself, for this curious child was very fond of pretending to be two people. "But it's no use now," thought poor Alice, "to pretend to be two people! Why, there's hardly enough of me left to make one respectable person!"

Soon her eye fell on a little glass box that was lying under the table: she opened it, and found in it a very small cake, on which the words "EAT ME" were beautifully marked in currants. "Well, I'll eat it," said Alice, "and if it makes me grow larger, I can reach the key; and if it makes me grow smaller, I can creep under the door: so either way I'll get into the garden, and I don't care which happens!"

She ate a little bit, and said anxiously to herself "Which way? Which way?" holding her hand on the top of her head to feel which way it was growing; and she was quite surprised to find that she remained the same size. To be sure, this is what generally happens when one eats cake; but Alice had got so much into the way of expecting nothing but out-of-the-way things to happen, that it seemed quite dull and stupid for life to go on in the common way. So she set to work, and very soon finished off the cake.

Name: _____

Reading Selection: _____

    1. What is the author's overall main idea, (central point, or thesis)?

_____

_____

    2. There are two kinds of supporting details--major and minor. Major details are the primary points that support the main idea and minor details expand major details. List three details and explain how they support the author's primary point?

Details used	Explanation of how they support the thesis
1.	

Details used	Explanation of how they support the thesis
2.	

Details used	Explanation of how they support the thesis
3.	

    3. The five main patterns of organization are the list of items pattern, the time order pattern, the example pattern, the comparison and/or contrast pattern, and the cause/effect pattern. What is the main pattern of organization used in this article? Explain why it is the main pattern. What other patterns are used? Give some examples.

Main pattern:

_____

Explain how the main pattern was used:

_____

_____

Write five of the transitions that helped indicate the main pattern of this selection:

_____ _____ _____ _____ _____

Other pattern(s) used:

_____

Explain how the additional pattern(s) were used:

_____
_____

What were some of the transitions that helped you to discover the other patterns?

_____ _____ _____ _____ _____

4. List <u>three</u> facts in the article. <u>Explain why</u> each it is a fact.

	Explanation:
A.) fact:	A.)
B.) fact:	B.)
C.) fact:	C.)

5. List <u>three</u> opinions in the article. <u>Explain why</u> each it is an opinion.

	Explanation:
A.) opinion	A.)
B.) opinion:	B.)
C.) opinion:	C.)

6. What is the author's main purpose in writing this article? Is it to inform, persuade, or entertain? <u>Tell me how you arrived at that conclusion.</u>

_____
_____
_____

7. What is the author's main tone? <u>Explain how you arrived at your answer.</u>

_____
_____
_____

Vocabulary Preview: These words may present challenges when reading. Preview them now, and return to them again if you need to.

Challenging words: A common definition:

1.	
2.	
3.	
4.	
5.	
6.	
7.	
8.	
9.	
10.	
11.	
12.	
13.	
14.	
15.	
16.	
17.	
18.	
19.	
20.	
21.	
22.	
23.	
24.	
25.	

Vocabulary Preview: These words may present challenges when reading. Preview them now, and return to them again if you need to.

Challenging words:	A common definition:
1.	
2.	
3.	
4.	
5.	
6.	
7.	
8.	
9.	
10.	
11.	
12.	
13.	
14.	
15.	
16.	
17.	
18.	
19.	
20.	
21.	
22.	
23.	
24.	
25.	

The Legend of Sleepy Hollow

By Washington Irving
1886

Commentary or Analysis:

**THE LEGEND OF SLEEPY HOLLOW
FOUND AMONG THE PAPERS OF THE LATE
DIEDRICH
KNICKERBOCKER**

A pleasing land of drowsy head it was,
Of dreams that wave before the half shut eye;
And of gay castles in the clouds that pass,
For ever flushing round a summer sky.
CASTLE OF INDOLENCE

In the bosom of one of those spacious coves which indent the eastern shore of the Hudson, at that broad expansion of the river denominated by the ancient Dutch navigators the Tappan Zee, and where they always prudently shortened sail, and implored the protection of St. Nicholas when they crossed, there lies a small market town or rural port, which by some is called Greensburgh, but which is more generally and properly known by the name of Tarry Town. This name was given, we are told, in former days, by the good housewives of the adjacent country, from the inveterate propensity of their husbands to linger about the village tavern on market days. Be that as it may, I do not vouch for the fact, but merely advert to it, for the sake of being precise and authentic. Not far from this village, perhaps about two miles, there is a little valley, or rather lap of land, among high hills, which is one of the quietest places in the whole world. A small brook glides through it, with just murmur enough to lull one to repose; and the occasional whistle of a quail or tapping of a woodpecker is almost the only sound that ever breaks in upon the uniform tranquility.

I recollect that, when a stripling, my first exploit in squirrel shooting was in a grove of tall walnut trees that shades one side of the valley. I had wandered into it at noontime, when all nature is peculiarly quiet, and was startled by the roar of my own gun, as it broke the Sabbath stillness around, and was prolonged and reverberated by the angry echoes. If ever I should wish for a retreat, whither I might steal from the world and its distractions and dream quietly away the remnant of a troubled life, I know of none more promising than this little valley.

From the listless repose of the place, and the peculiar character of its inhabitants, who are descendants from the original Dutch settlers, this sequestered glen has long been known by the name of SLEEPY HOLLOW, and its rustic lads are called the Sleepy Hollow Boys throughout all the neighboring country. A drowsy, dreamy influence seems to hang over the land, and to pervade the very atmosphere. Some say that the place was bewitched by a high German doctor during the early days of the settlement; others, that an old Indian chief, the prophet or wizard of his tribe, held his powwows there before the country was discovered by Master Hendrick Hudson. Certain it is, the place still continues under the sway of some witching power that holds a spell over the minds of the good people, causing them to walk in a continual reverie. They are given to all kinds of marvelous beliefs, are subject to trances and visions, and frequently see strange sights, and hear music and voices in the air. The whole neighborhood abounds with local tales, haunted spots, and twilight superstitions; stars shoot and meteors glare oftener across the valley than in any other part of the country, and the nightmare, with her whole ninefold, seems to make it the favorite scene of her gambols.

The dominant spirit, however, that haunts this enchanted region and seems to be commander-in-chief of all the powers of the air is the apparition of a figure on horseback without a head. It is said by some to be the ghost of a Hessian trooper, whose head had been carried away by a cannon ball, in some nameless battle during the Revolutionary War, and who is ever and anon seen by the country folk, hurrying along in the gloom of night, as if on the wings of the wind. His haunts are not confined to the valley, but extend at times to the adjacent roads, and especially to the vicinity of a church at no great distance. Indeed, certain of the most authentic historians of those parts, who have been careful in collecting and collating the floating facts concerning this specter, allege that the body of the trooper, having been buried in the churchyard, the ghost rides forth to the scene of battle in nightly quest of his head; and that the rushing speed with which he sometimes passes along the Hollow, like a midnight blast, is owing to his being belated, and in a hurry to get back to the churchyard before daybreak.

Such is the general purport of this legendary superstition, which has furnished materials for many a wild story in that region of shadows; and the specter is known, at all the country firesides, by the name of the Headless Horseman of Sleepy Hollow.

It is remarkable that the visionary propensity I have mentioned is not confined to the native inhabitants of the valley, but is unconsciously imbibed by everyone who resides there for a time. However wide awake they may have been before they entered that sleepy region, they are sure, in a little time, to inhale the witching influence of the air, and begin to grow imaginative -- to dream dreams and see apparitions.

I mention this peaceful spot with all possible laud; for it is in such little retired Dutch valleys, found here and there embosomed in the great State of New York, that population, manners, and customs remain fixed; while the great torrent of migration and improvement, which is making such incessant changes in other parts of this restless country, sweeps by them unobserved. They are like those little nooks of still water which border a rapid stream, where we may see the straw and bubble riding quietly at anchor, or slowly revolving in their mimic harbor, undisturbed by the rush of the passing current. Though many years have elapsed since I trod the drowsy shades of Sleepy Hollow, yet I question whether I should not still find the same trees and the same families vegetating in its sheltered bosom.

In this by-place of nature there abode, in a remote period

of American history, that is to say, some thirty years since, a worthy wight of the name of Ichabod Crane, who sojourned, or, as he expressed it, "tarried," in Sleepy Hollow, for the purpose of instructing the children of the vicinity. He was a native of Connecticut, a State which supplies the Union with pioneers for the mind as well as for the forest, and sends forth yearly its legions of frontier woodsmen and country schoolmasters. The cognomen of Crane was not inapplicable to his person. He was tall, but exceedingly lank, with narrow shoulders, long arms and legs, hands that dangled a mile out of his sleeves, feet that might have served for shovels, and his whole frame most loosely hung together. His head was small, and flat at top, with huge ears, large green glassy eyes, and a long snipe nose, so that it looked like a weathercock, perched upon his spindle neck, to tell which way the wind blew. To see him striding along the profile of a hill on a windy day, with his clothes bagging and fluttering about him, one might have mistaken him for the genius of famine descending upon the earth, or some scarecrow eloped from a cornfield.

His schoolhouse was a low building of one large room, rudely constructed of logs, the windows partly glazed, and partly patched with leaves of old copybooks. It was most ingeniously secured at vacant hours by a withe twisted in the handle of the door and stakes set against the window shutters, so that, though a thief might get in with perfect ease, he would find some embarrassment in getting out; an idea most probably borrowed by the architect, Yost Van Houten, from the mystery of an eel pot. The schoolhouse stood in a rather lonely but pleasant situation, just at the foot of a woody hill, with a brook running close by, and a formidable birch tree growing at one end of it. From hence the low murmur of his pupils' voices, conning over their lessons, might be heard in a drowsy summer's day, like the hum of a beehive, interrupted now and then by the authoritative voice of the master, in the tone of menace or command, or, peradventure, by the appalling sound of the birch, as he urged some tardy loiterer along the flowery path of knowledge. Truth to say, he was a conscientious man, and ever bore in mind the golden maxim, "Spare the rod and spoil the child." Ichabod Crane's scholars certainly were not spoiled.

I would not have it imagined, however, that he was one of those cruel potentates of the school who joy in the smart of their subjects; on the contrary, he administered justice with discrimination rather than severity, taking the burthen off the backs of the weak, and laying it on those of the strong. Your mere puny stripling that winced at the least flourish of the rod was passed by with indulgence; but the claims of justice were satisfied by inflicting a double portion on some little, tough, wrong-headed, broad-skirted Dutch urchin, who sulked and swelled and grew dogged and sullen beneath the birch. All this he called "doing his duty by their parents"; and he never inflicted a chastisement without following it by the assurance, so consolatory to the smarting urchin, that "he would remember it, and thank him for it the longest day he had to live."

When school hours were over, he was even the companion and playmate of the larger boys; and on holiday afternoons would convoy some of the smaller ones home, who happened to have pretty sisters, or good housewives for mothers, noted for the comforts of the cupboard. Indeed it behooved him to keep on good terms with his pupils. The revenue arising from his school was small, and would have been scarcely sufficient to furnish him with daily bread, for he was a huge feeder, and though lank, had the dilating powers of an anaconda; but to help out his maintenance, he was, according to country custom in those parts, boarded and lodged at the houses of the farmers whose children he instructed. With these he lived successively a week at a time; thus going the rounds of the neighborhood, with all his worldly effects tied up in a cotton handkerchief.

That all this might not be too onerous on the purses of his rustic patrons, who are apt to consider the costs of schooling a grievous burden and schoolmasters as mere drones, he had various ways of rendering himself both useful and agreeable. He assisted the farmers occasionally in the lighter labors of their farms, helped to make hay, mended the fences, took the horses to water, drove the cows from pasture, and cut wood for the winter

149

fire. He laid aside, too, all the dominant dignity and absolute sway with which he lorded it in his little empire, the school, and became wonderfully gentle and ingratiating. He found favor in the eyes of the mothers by petting the children, particularly the youngest; and like the lion bold, which whilom so magnanimously the lamb did hold, he would sit with a child on one knee, and rock a cradle with his foot for whole hours together.

In addition to his other vocations, he was the singing master of the neighborhood, and picked up many bright shillings by instructing the young folks in psalmody. It was a matter of no little vanity to him, on Sundays, to take his station in front of the church gallery, with a band of chosen singers; where, in his own mind, he completely carried away the palm from the parson. Certain it is, his voice resounded far above all the rest of the congregation; and there are peculiar quavers still to be heard in that church, and which may even be heard half a mile off, quite to the opposite side of the millpond, on a still Sunday morning, which are said to be legitimately descended from the nose of Ichabod Crane. Thus, by diverse little makeshifts in that ingenious way which is commonly denominated "by hook and by crook," the worthy pedagogue got on tolerably enough, and was thought, by all who understood nothing of the labor of headwork, to have a wonderfully easy life of it.

The schoolmaster is generally a man of some importance in the female circle of a rural neighborhood, being considered a kind of idle gentlemanlike personage, of vastly superior taste and accomplishments to the rough country swains, and, indeed, inferior in learning only to the parson. His appearance, therefore, is apt to occasion some little stir at the tea table of a farmhouse, and the addition of a supernumerary dish of cakes or sweetmeats, or, peradventure, the parade of a silver teapot. Our man of letters, therefore, was peculiarly happy in the smiles of all the country damsels. How he would figure among them in the churchyard, between services on Sundays! gathering grapes for them from the wild vines that overrun the surrounding trees, reciting for their amusement all the epitaphs on the tombstones, or sauntering, with a whole bevy of them, along the banks of the adjacent millpond, while the more bashful country

150

bumpkins hung sheepishly back, envying his superior elegance and address.

From his half-itinerant life, also, he was a kind of traveling gazette, carrying the whole budget of local gossip from house to house, so that his appearance was always greeted with satisfaction. He was, moreover, esteemed by the women as a man of his great erudition, for he had read several books quite through, and was a perfect master of Cotton Mather's History of New England Witchcraft, in which, by the way, he most firmly and potently believed.

He was, in fact, an odd mixture of small shrewdness and simple credulity. His appetite for the marvelous, and his powers of digesting it, were equally extraordinary; and both had been increased by his residence in this spellbound region. No tale was too gross or monstrous for his capacious swallow. It was often his delight, after his school was dismissed in the afternoon, to stretch himself on the rich bed of clover, bordering the little brook that whimpered by his schoolhouse, and there con over old Mather's direful tales, until the gathering dusk of the evening made the printed page a mere mist before his eyes. Then, as he wended his way, by swamp and stream and awful woodland, to the farmhouse where he happened to be quartered, every sound of nature, at that witching hour, fluttered his excited imagination: the moan of the whip-poor-will from the hillside; the boding cry of the tree toad, that harbinger of storm; the dreary hooting of the screech owl, or the sudden rustling in the thicket of birds frightened from their roost. The fireflies, too, which sparkled most vividly in the darkest places, now and then startled him, as one of uncommon brightness would stream across his path; and if, by chance, a huge blockhead of a beetle came winging his blundering flight against him, the poor varlet was ready to give up the ghost, with the idea that he was struck with a witch's token. His only resource on such occasions, either to drown thought or drive away evil spirits, was to sing psalm tunes; and the good people of Sleepy Hollow, as they sat by their doors of an evening, were often filled with awe, at hearing his nasal melody, "in linked sweetness long drawn out," floating from the distant hill or

151

along the dusky road.

Another of his sources of fearful pleasure was to pass long winter evenings with the old Dutch wives as they sat spinning by the fire, with a row of apples roasting and spluttering along the hearth, and listen to their marvelous tales of ghosts and goblins, and haunted fields, and haunted brooks, and haunted bridges, and haunted houses, and particularly of the headless horseman, or galloping Hessian of the Hollow, as they sometimes called him. He would delight them equally by his anecdotes of witchcraft, and of the direful omens and portentous sights and sounds in the air, which prevailed in the earlier times of Connecticut; and would frighten them woefully with speculations upon comets and shooting stars, and with the alarming fact that the world did absolutely turn around, and that they were half the time topsy-turvy!

But if there was a pleasure in all this, while snugly cuddling in the chimney corner of a chamber that was all of a ruddy glow from the crackling wood fire, and where, of course, no specter dared to show his face, it was dearly purchased by the terrors of his subsequent walk homewards. What fearful shapes and shadows beset his path amidst the dim and ghastly glare of a snowy night! With what wistful look did he eye every trembling ray of light streaming across the waste fields from some distant window! How often was he appalled by some shrub covered with snow, which, like a sheeted specter, beset his very path! How often did he shrink with curdling awe at the sound of his own steps on the frosty crust beneath his feet; and dread to look over his shoulder, lest he should behold some uncouth being tramping close behind him! And how often was he thrown into complete dismay by some rushing blast, howling among the trees, in the idea that it was the Galloping Hessian on one of his nightly scourings!

All these, however, were mere terrors of the night, phantoms of the mind that walk in darkness; and though he had seen many specters in his time, and been more than once beset by Satan in diverse shapes, in his lonely perambulations, yet daylight put an end to all these evils,

152

and he would have passed a pleasant life of it, in despite of the devil and all his works, if his path had not been crossed by a being that causes more perplexity to mortal man than ghosts, goblins, and the whole race of witches put together, and that was -- a woman.

Among the musical disciples who assembled, one evening in each week, to receive his instructions in psalmody, was Katrina Van Tassel, the daughter and only child of a substantial Dutch farmer. She was a blooming lass of fresh eighteen, plump as a partridge, ripe and melting and rosy-cheeked as one of her father's peaches, and universally famed not merely for her beauty, but her vast expectations. She was withal a little of a coquette, as might be perceived even in her dress, which was a mixture of ancient and modern fashions, as most suited to set off her charms. She wore the ornaments of pure yellow gold, which her great-great-grandmother had brought over from Saardam; the tempting stomacher of the olden time; and withal a provokingly short petticoat, to display the prettiest foot and ankle in the country around.

Ichabod Crane had a soft and foolish heart toward the sex; and it is not to be wondered at that so tempting a morsel soon found favor in his eyes, more especially after he had visited her in her paternal mansion. Old Baltus Van Tassel was a perfect picture of a thriving, contented, liberal-hearted farmer. He seldom, it is true, sent either his eyes or his thoughts beyond the boundaries of his own farm; but within those everything was snug, happy, and well-conditioned. He was satisfied with his wealth, but not proud of it; and piqued himself upon the hearty abundance, rather than the style in which he lived. His stronghold was situated on the banks of the Hudson, in one of those green, sheltered, fertile nooks, in which the Dutch farmers are so fond of nestling. A great elm tree spread its broad branches over it, at the foot of which bubbled up a spring of the softest and sweetest water, in a little well, formed of a barrel, and then stole sparkling away through the grass, to a neighboring brook that bubbled along among alders and dwarf willows. Hard by the farmhouse was a vast barn that might have served for a church; every window and crevice of which seemed bursting forth with the treasures of the farm; the flail

153

was busily resounding within it from morning to night; swallows and martins skimmed twittering about the eaves; and rows of pigeons, some with one eye turned up, as if watching the weather, some with their heads' under their wings, or buried in their bosoms, and others swelling, and cooing, and bowing about their dames, were enjoying the sunshine on the roof. Sleek unwieldy porkers were grunting in the repose and abundance of their pens; whence sallied forth, now and then, troops of sucking pigs, as if to snuff the air. A stately squadron of snowy geese were riding in an adjoining pond, convoying whole fleets of ducks; regiments of turkeys were gobbling through the farmyard, and guinea fowls fretting about it, like ill-tempered housewives, with their peevish discontented cry. Before the barn door strutted the gallant cock, that pattern of a husband, a warrior, and a fine gentleman, clapping his burnished wings and crowing in the pride and gladness of his heart -- sometimes tearing up the earth with his feet, and then generously calling his ever-hungry family of wives and children to enjoy the rich morsel which he had discovered.

The pedagogue's mouth watered as he looked upon this sumptuous promise of luxurious winter fare. In his devouring mind's eye he pictured to himself every roasting pig running about with a pudding in his belly and an apple in his mouth; the pigeons were snugly put to bed in a comfortable pie, and tucked in with a coverlet of crust; the geese were swimming in their own gravy; and the ducks pairing cozily in dishes, like snug married couples, with a decent competency of onion sauce. In the porkers he saw carved out the future sleek side of bacon, and juicy relishing ham; not a turkey but he behold daintily trussed up, with its gizzard under its wing, and, peradventure, a necklace of savory sausages; and even bright chanticleer himself lay sprawling on his back, in a sidedish, with uplifted claws, as if craving that quarter which his chivalrous spirit disdained to ask while living.

As the enraptured Ichabod fancied all this, and as he rolled his great green eyes over the fat meadow lands, the rich fields of wheat, of rye, of buckwheat, and Indian corn, and the orchards burthened with ruddy fruit, which surrounded the warm tenement of Van Tassel, his heart yearned after the damsel who was to inherit these domains, and his imagination expanded with the idea how they might be readily turned into cash, and the money invested in immense tracts of wild land, and shingle palaces in the wilderness. Nay, his busy fancy already realized his hopes, and presented to him the blooming Katrina, with a whole family of children, mounted on the top of a wagon loaded with household trumpery, with pots and kettles dangling beneath; and he beheld himself bestriding a pacing mare, with a colt at her heels, setting out for Kentucky, Tennessee, or the Lord knows where.

When he entered the house the conquest of his heart was complete. It was one of those spacious farmhouses, with high-ridged, but lowly sloping roofs, built in the style handed down from the first Dutch settlers, the low projecting eaves forming a piazza along the front, capable of being closed up in bad weather. Under this were hung flails, harness, various utensils of husbandry, and nets for fishing in the neighboring river. Benches were built along the sides for summer use; and a great spinning wheel at one end, and a churn at the other, showed the various uses to which this important porch might be devoted. From this piazza the wondering Ichabod entered the hall, which formed the center of the mansion and the place of usual residence. Here, rows of resplendent pewter, ranged on a long dresser, dazzled his eyes. In one corner stood a huge bag of wool ready to be spun; in another a quantity of linsey-woolsey just from the loom; ears of Indian corn and strings of dried apples and peaches hung in gay festoons along the walls, mingled with the gaud of red peppers; and a door left ajar gave him a peep into the best parlor, where the claw-footed chairs and dark mahogany tables shone like mirrors; and irons, with their accompanying shovel and tongs, glistened from their covert of asparagus tops; mock oranges and conch shells decorated the mantel-piece; strings of various colored birds' eggs were suspended above it; a great ostrich egg was hung from the center of the room, and a corner cupboard, knowingly left open, displayed immense treasures of old silver and well-mended china.

155

From the moment Ichabod laid his eyes upon these regions of delight, the peace of his mind was at an end, and his only study was how to gain the affections of the peerless daughter of Van Tassel. In this enterprise, however, he had more real difficulties than generally fell to the lot of a knight-errant of yore, who seldom had anything but giants, enchanters, fiery dragons, and such like easily conquered adversaries to contend with; and had to make his way merely through gates of iron and brass, and walls of adamant, to the castle keep, where the lady of his heart was confined; all which he achieved as easily as a man would carve his way to the center of a Christmas pie; and then the lady gave him her hand as a matter of course. Ichabod, on the contrary, had to win his way to the heart of a country coquette, beset with a labyrinth of whims and caprices, which were forever presenting new difficulties and impediments; and he had to encounter a host of fearful adversaries of real flesh and blood, the numerous rustic admirers, who beset every portal to her heart, keeping a watchful and angry eye upon each other, but ready to fly out in the common cause against any new competitor.

Among these the most formidable was a burly, roaring, roystering blade, of the name of Abraham, or, according to the Dutch abbreviation, Brom Van Brunt, the hero of the country round, which rang with his feats of strength and hardihood. He was broad-shouldered and double-jointed, with short curly black hair, and a bluff but not unpleasant countenance, having a mingled air of fun and arrogance. From his Herculean frame and great powers of limb, he had received the nickname of BROM BONES, by which he was universally known. He was famed for great knowledge and skill in horsemanship, being as dexterous on horseback as a Tartar. He was foremost at all races and cockfights; and, with the ascendency which bodily strength acquires in rustic life, was the umpire in all disputes, setting his hat on one side and giving his decisions with an air and tone admitting of no gainsay or appeal. He was always ready for either a fight or a frolic; but had more mischief than ill will in his composition, and, with all his overbearing roughness, there was a strong dash of waggish good humor at bottom. He had three or four boon companions, who regarded him as their model and at the head of whom he scoured the country, attending every scene of feud or merriment for miles around. In cold weather he was distinguished by a fur cap, surmounted with a flaunting fox's tail; and when the folks at a country gathering descried this well-known crest at a distance, whisking about among a squad of hard riders, they always stood by for a squall. Sometimes his crew would be heard dashing along past the farmhouses at midnight, with whoop and halloo, like a troop of Don Cossacks; and the old dames, startled out of their sleep, would listen for a moment till the hurry-scurry had clattered by, and then exclaim, "Ay, there goes Brom Bones and his gang!" The neighbors looked upon him with a mixture of awe, admiration, and good will; and when any madcap prank or rustic brawl occurred in the vicinity, always shook their heads and warranted Brom Bones was at the bottom of it.

This rantipole hero had for some time singled out the blooming Katrina for the object of his uncouth gallantries, and though his amorous toyings were something like the gentle caresses and endearments of a bear, yet it was whispered that she did not altogether discourage his hopes. Certain it is, his advances were signals for rival candidates to retire, who felt no inclination to cross a lion in his amours; insomuch, that when his horse was seen tied to Van Tassel's paling, on a Sunday night, a sure sign that his master was courting, or, as it is termed, "sparking," within, all other suitors passed by in despair, and carried the war into other quarters.

Such was the formidable rival with whom Ichabod Crane had to contend, and, considering all things, a stouter man than he would have shrunk from the competition, and a wiser man would have despaired. He had, however, a happy mixture of pliability and perseverance in his nature; he was in form and spirit like a supple jack -- yielding, but tough; though he bent, he never broke; and though he bowed beneath the slightest pressure, yet, the moment it was away -- jerk! he was as erect, and carried his head as high as ever.

To have taken the field openly against his rival would have been madness, for he was not a man to be thwarted in his amours, any more than that stormy lover Achilles. Ichabod, therefore, made his advances in a quiet and gently insinuating manner. Under cover of his character of singing master, he made frequent visits to the farmhouse; not that he had anything to apprehend from the meddlesome interference of parents, which is so often a stumbling block in the path of lovers. Balt Van Tassel was an easy indulgent soul; he loved his daughter better even than his pipe, and, like a reasonable man and an excellent father, let her have her way in everything. His notable little wife, too, had enough to do to attend to her housekeeping and manage her poultry; for, as she sagely observed, ducks and geese are foolish things, and must be looked after, but girls can take care of themselves. Thus while the busy dame bustled about the house, or plied her spinning wheel at one end of the piazza, honest Balt would sit smoking his evening pipe at the other, watching the achievements of a little wooden warrior, who, armed with a sword in each hand, was most valiantly fighting the wind on the pinnacle of the barn. In the meantime, Ichabod would carry on his suit with the daughter by the side of the spring under the great elm, or sauntering along in the twilight, that hour so favorable to the lover's eloquence.

I profess not to know how women's hearts are wooed and won. To me they have always been matters of riddle and admiration. Some seem to have but one vulnerable point, or door of access, while others have a thousand avenues, and may be captured in a thousand different ways. It is a great triumph of skill to gain the former, but a still greater proof of generalship to maintain possession of the latter, for the man must battle for his fortress at every door and window. He who wins a thousand common hearts is therefore entitled to some renown; but he who keeps undisputed sway over the heart of a coquette is indeed a hero. Certain it is, this was not the case with the redoubtable Brom Bones; and from the moment Ichabod Crane made his advances, the interests of the former evidently declined; his horse was no longer seen tied at the palings on Sunday nights, and a deadly feud gradually arose between him and the preceptor of Sleepy Hollow.

Brom, who had a degree of rough chivalry in his nature, would fain have carried matters to open warfare, and have settled their pretensions to the lady according to the mode of those most concise and simple reasoners, the knights-errant of yore -- by single combat; but Ichabod was too conscious of the superior might of his adversary to enter the lists against him. He had overheard a boast of Bones that he would "double the schoolmaster up, and lay him on a shelf of his own schoolhouse," and he was too wary to give him an opportunity. There was something extremely provoking in this obstinately pacific system; it left Brom no alternative but to draw upon the funds of rustic waggery in his disposition, and to play off boorish practical jokes upon his rival. Ichabod became the object of whimsical persecution to Bones and his gang of rough riders. They harried his hitherto peaceful domains; smoked out his singing school by stopping up the chimney; broke into the schoolhouse at night, in spite of its formidable fastenings of withe and window stakes, and turned everything topsy-turvy, so that the poor schoolmaster began to think all the witches in the country held their meetings there. But what was still more annoying, Brom took all opportunities of turning him into ridicule in presence of his mistress, and had a scoundrel dog whom he taught to whine in the most ludicrous manner, and introduced as a rival of Ichabod's to instruct her in psalmody.

In this way matters went on for sometime, without producing any material effect on the relative situation of the contending powers. On a fine autumnal afternoon, Ichabod, in pensive mood, sat enthroned on the lofty stool whence he usually watched all the concerns of his little literary realm. In his hand he swayed a ferule, that scepter of despotic power; the birch of justice reposed on three nails, behind the throne, a constant terror to evil-doers; while on the desk before him might be seen sundry contraband articles and prohibited weapons, detected upon the persons of idle urchins, such as half-munched apples, popguns, whirligigs, fly cages, and whole legions of rampant little paper gamecocks. Apparently there had been some appalling act of justice recently inflicted, for his scholars were all busily intent upon their books, or slyly whispering behind them with one eye kept upon the master; and a kind of buzzing stillness reigned throughout the school- room. It was suddenly interrupted by the appearance of a Negro, in tow-cloth jacket and trousers, a round-crowned fragment of a hat, like the cap of Mercury, and mounted on the back of a ragged, wild, half-broken colt, which he managed with a rope by way of halter. He came clattering up to the school door with an invitation to Ichabod to attend a merrymaking or "quilting frolic" to be held that evening at Mynheer Van Tassel's; and having delivered his message with that air of importance and effort at fine language which a Negro is apt to display on petty embassies of the kind, he dashed over the brook and was seen scampering away up the hollow, full of the importance and hurry of his mission.

All was now bustle and hubbub in the late quiet schoolroom. The scholars were hurried through their lessons, without stopping at trifles; those who were nimble skipped over half with impunity, and those who were tardy had a smart application now and then in the rear to quicken their speed or help them over a tall word. Books were flung aside without being put away on the shelves, ink-stands were overturned, benches thrown down, and the whole school was turned loose an hour before the usual time, bursting forth like a legion of young imps, yelping and racketing about the green, in joy at their early emancipation.

The gallant Ichabod now spent at least an extra half hour at his toilet, brushing and furbishing up his best and indeed only suit of rusty black, and arranging his looks by a bit of broken looking glass that hung up in the schoolhouse. That he might make his appearance before his mistress in the true style of a cavalier he borrowed a horse from the farmer with whom he was domiciliated, a choleric old Dutchman of the name of Hans Van Ripper, and, thus gallantly mounted, issued forth, like a knight-errant in quest of adventures. But it is meet I should, in the true spirit of romantic story, give some account of the looks and equipments of my hero and his steed. The animal he bestrode was a broken-down plow horse that had outlived almost everything but his viciousness. He was gaunt and shagged, with a ewe neck and a head like a hammer; his rusty mane and tail were tangled and knotted with burrs; one eye had lost its pupil and was glaring and spectral, but the other had the gleam of a genuine devil in it. Still he must have had fire and mettle in his day, if we may judge from the name he bore of Gunpowder. He had, in fact, been a favorite steed of his master's, the choleric Van Ripper, who was a furious rider, and had infused, very probably, some of his own spirit into the animal, for, old and broken-down as he looked, there was more of the lurking devil in him than in any young filly in the country.

Ichabod was a suitable figure for such a steed. He rode with short stirrups, which brought his knees nearly up to the pommel of the saddle; his sharp elbows stuck out like grasshoppers'; he carried his whip perpendicularly in his hand, like a scepter, and, as his horse jogged on, the motion of his arms was not unlike the flapping of a pair of wings. A small wool hat rested on the top of his nose, for so his scanty strip of forehead might be called; and the skirts of his black coat fluttered out almost to the horse's tail. Such was the appearance of Ichabod and his steed, as they shambled out of the gate of Hans Van Ripper, and it was altogether such an apparition as is seldom to be met with in broad daylight.

It was, as I have said, a fine autumnal day, the sky was clear and serene, and nature wore that rich and golden livery which we always associate with the idea of abundance. The forests had put on their sober brown and yellow, while some trees of the tenderer kind had been nipped by the frosts into brilliant dyes of orange, purple, and scarlet. Streaming files of wild ducks began to make their appearance high in the air; the bark of the squirrel might be heard from the groves of beech and hickory nuts, and the pensive whistle of the quail at intervals from the neighboring stubble field.

The small birds were taking their farewell banquets. In the fullness of their revelry, they fluttered, chirping and frolicking, from bush to bush, and tree to tree, capricious from the very profusion and variety around them. There was the honest cock robin, the favorite game of stripling sportsmen, with its loud querulous note; and the twittering blackbirds flying in sable clouds; and the golden-winged woodpecker, with his crimson crest, his broad black gorget, and splendid plumage; and the cedar bird, with its red-tipped wings and yellow-tipped tail, and its little monteiro cap of feathers; and the blue jay, that noisy coxcomb, in his gay light-blue coat and white underclothes; screaming and chattering, nodding and bobbing and bowing, and pretending to be on good terms with every songster of the grove.

As Ichabod jogged slowly on his way, his eye, ever open to every symptom of culinary abundance, ranged with delight over the treasures of jolly autumn. On all sides he beheld vast store of apples, some hanging in oppressive opulence on the trees, some gathered into baskets and barrels for the market, others heaped up in rich piles for the cider press. Farther on he beheld great fields of Indian corn, with its golden ears peeping from their leafy coverts and holding out the promise of cakes and hasty pudding; and the yellow pumpkins lying beneath them, turning up their fair round bellies to the sun, and giving ample prospects of the most luxurious of pies; and anon he passed the fragrant buckwheat fields, breathing the odor of the beehive, and as he beheld them, soft anticipations stole over his mind of dainty slapjacks, well buttered and garnished with honey or treacle, by the delicate little dimpled hand of Katrina Van Tassel.

Thus feeding his mind with many sweet thoughts and "sugared suppositions," he journeyed along the sides of a range of hills which look out upon some of the goodliest scenes of the mighty Hudson. The sun gradually wheeled his broad disk down into the west. The wide bosom of the Tappan Zee lay motionless and glassy, excepting that here and there a gentle undulation waved and prolonged the blue shadow of the distant mountain. A few amber clouds floated in the sky, without a breath of air to move them. The horizon was of a fine golden tint, changing gradually into a pure apple green, and from that into the deep blue of the mid-heaven. A slanting ray lingered on the woody crests of the precipices that overhung some parts of the river, giving greater depth to the dark-gray and purple of their rocky sides. A sloop was loitering in the distance, dropping slowly down with the tide, her sail

162

hanging uselessly against the mast; and as the reflection of the sky gleamed along the still water, it seemed as if the vessel was suspended in the air.

It was toward evening that Ichabod arrived at the castle of the Heer Van Tassel, which he found thronged with the pride and flower of the adjacent country. Old farmers, a spare leathern-faced race, in homespun coats and breeches, blue stockings, huge shoes, and magnificent pewter buckles. Their brisk withered little dames, in close-crimped caps, long-waisted short gowns, homespun petticoats, with scissors and pincushions and gay calico pockets hanging on the outside. Buxom lasses, almost as antiquated as their mothers, excepting where a straw hat, a fine ribbon, or perhaps a white frock gave symptoms of city innovation. The sons, in short square-skirted coats with rows of stupendous brass buttons, and their hair generally queued in the fashion of the times, especially if they could procure an eel skin for the purpose, it being esteemed throughout the country as a potent nourisher and strengthener of the hair.

Brom Bones, however, was the hero of the scene, having come to the gathering on his favorite steed Daredevil, a creature, like himself, full of mettle and mischief, and which no one but himself could manage. He was, in fact, noted for preferring vicious animals, given to all kinds of tricks, which kept the rider in constant risk of his neck, for he held a tractable well-broken horse as unworthy of a lad of spirit.

Fain would I pause to dwell upon the world of charms that burst upon the enraptured gaze of my hero as he entered the state parlor of Van Tassel's mansion. Not those of the bevy of buxom lasses, with their luxurious display of red and white, but the ample charms of a genuine Dutch country tea-table, in the sumptuous time of autumn. Such heaped-up platters of cakes of various and almost indescribable kinds, known only to experienced Dutch housewives! There was the doughty doughnut, the tenderer oly koek, and the crisp and crumbling cruller; sweet cakes and shortcakes, ginger cakes and honey cakes, and the whole family of cakes. And then there were apple pies and peach pies and pumpkin pies;

besides slices of ham and smoked beef; and moreover delectable dishes of preserved plums, and peaches, and pears, and quinces; not to mention broiled shad and roasted chickens; together with bowls of milk and cream, all mingled higgledy-piggledy, pretty much as I have enumerated them, with the motherly teapot sending up its clouds of vapor from the midst -- Heaven bless the mark! I want breath and time to discuss this banquet as it deserves, and am too eager to get on with my story. Happily, Ichabod Crane was not in so great a hurry as his historian, but did ample justice to every dainty.

He was a kind and thankful creature whose heart dilated in proportion as his skin was filled with good cheer, and whose spirits rose with eating as some men's do with drink. He could not help, too, rolling his large eyes around him as he ate, and chuckling with the possibility that he might one day be lord of all this scene of almost unimaginable luxury and splendor. Then, he thought, how soon he'd turn his back upon the old schoolhouse; snap his fingers in the face of Hans Van Ripper, and every other niggardly patron, and kick any itinerant pedagogue out of doors that should dare to call him comrade!

Old Baltus Van Tassel moved about among his guests with a face dilated with content and good humor, round and jolly as the harvest moon. His hospitable attentions were brief, but expressive, being confined to a shake of the hand, a slap on the shoulder, a loud laugh, and a pressing invitation to "fall to, and help themselves."

And now the sound of the music from the common room, or hall, summoned to the dance. The musician was an old gray-headed Negro, who had been the itinerant orchestra of the neighborhood for more than half a century. His instrument was as old and battered as himself. The greater part of the time he scraped on two or three strings, accompanying every movement of the bow with a motion of the head; bowing almost to the ground and stamping with his foot whenever a fresh couple were to start.

Ichabod prided himself upon his dancing as much as upon his vocal powers. Not a limb, not a fiber about him was idle; and to have seen his loosely hung frame in full motion, and clattering about the room, you would have thought Saint Vitus himself, that blessed patron of the dance, was figuring before you in person. He was the admiration of all the Negroes, who, having gathered, of all ages and sizes, from the farm and the neighborhood, stood forming a pyramid of shining black faces at every door and window, gazing with delight at the scene, rolling their white eyeballs, and showing grinning rows of ivory from ear to ear. How could the flogger of urchins be otherwise than animated and joyous? The lady of his heart was his partner in the dance, and smiling graciously in reply to all his amorous oglings, while Brom Bones, sorely smitten with love and jealousy, sat brooding by himself in one corner.

When the dance was at an end, Ichabod was attracted to a knot of the sager folks, who, with old Van Tassel, sat smoking at one end of the piazza, gossiping over former times, and drawing out long stories about the war.
This neighborhood, at the time of which I am speaking, was one of those highly favored places which abound with chronicle and great men. The British and American line had run near it during the war; it had, therefore, been the scene of marauding, and infested with refugees, cowboys, and all kinds of border chivalry. Just sufficient time had elapsed to enable each storyteller to dress up his tale with a little becoming fiction, and, in the indistinctness of his recollection, to make himself the hero of every exploit.

There was the story of Doffue Martling, a large blue-bearded Dutchman, who had nearly taken a British frigate with an old iron nine-pounder from a mud breastwork, only that his gun burst at the sixth discharge. And there was an old gentleman who shall be nameless, being too rich a mynheer to be lightly mentioned, who, in the Battle of White Plains, being an excellent master of defense, parried a musket ball with a small sword, insomuch that he absolutely felt it whiz around the blade and glance off at the hilt, in proof of which he was ready at any time to show the sword, with the hilt a little bent. There were several more that had been equally great in the field, not one of whom but was persuaded that he had a considerable hand in bringing the war to a happy termination.

But all these were nothing to the tales of ghosts and apparitions that succeeded. The neighborhood is rich in legendary treasures of the kind. Local tales and superstitions thrive best in these sheltered long-settled retreats, but are trampled under foot by the shifting throng that forms the population of most of our country places. Besides, there is no encouragement for ghosts in most of our villages, for they have scarcely had time to finish their first nap and turn themselves in their graves before their surviving friends have traveled away from the neighborhood; so that when they turn out at night to walk their rounds they have no acquaintance left to call upon. This is perhaps the reason why we so seldom hear of ghosts except in our long-established Dutch communities.

The immediate cause, however, of the prevalence of supernatural stories in these parts was doubtless owing to the vicinity of Sleepy Hollow. There was a contagion in the very air that blew from that haunted region; it breathed forth an atmosphere of dreams and fancies infecting all the land. Several of the Sleepy Hollow people were present at Van Tassel's, and, as usual, were doling out their wild and wonderful legends Many dismal tales were told about funeral trains, and mourning cries and wailings heard and seen about the great tree where the unfortunate Major Andre was taken, and which stood in the neighborhood. Some mention was made also of the woman in white that haunted the dark glen at Raven Rock, and was often heard to shriek on winter nights before a storm, having perished there in the snow. The chief part of the stories, however, turned upon the favorite specter of Sleepy Hollow, the headless horseman, who had been heard several times of late, patrolling the country, and, it was said, tethered his horse nightly among the graves in the churchyard.

The sequestered situation of this church seems always to have made it a favorite haunt of troubled spirits. It stands on a knoll, surrounded by locust trees and lofty elms, from among which its decent whitewashed walls shine modestly forth, like Christian purity beaming through the shades of retirement. A gentle slope descends from it to a silver sheet of water, bordered by high trees, between which peeps may be caught at the blue hills of the Hudson. To look upon its grass-grown yard, where the sunbeams seem to sleep so quietly, one would think that there at least the dead might rest in peace. On one side of the church extends a wide woody dell, along which raves a large brook among broken rocks and trunks of fallen trees. Over a deep black part of the stream, not far from the church, was formerly thrown a wooden bridge; the road that led to it, and the bridge itself, were thickly shaded by overhanging trees, which cast a gloom about it, even in the daytime, but occasioned a fearful darkness at night. This was one of the favorite haunts of the headless horseman, and the place where he was most frequently encountered. The tale was told of old Brouwer, a most heretical disbeliever in ghosts, how he met the horseman returning from his foray into Sleepy Hollow, and was obliged to get up behind him; how they galloped over bush and brake, over hill and swamp, until they reached the bridge, when the horseman suddenly turned into a skeleton, threw old Brouwer into the brook, and sprang away over the treetops with a clap of thunder.

This story was immediately matched by a thrice marvelous adventure of Brom Bones, who made light of the galloping Hessian as an arrant jockey. He affirmed that, on returning one night from the neighboring village of Sing Sing, he had been overtaken by this midnight trooper; that he had offered to race with him for a bowl of punch, and should have won it too, for Daredevil beat the goblin horse all hollow, but, just as they came to the church bridge, the Hessian bolted and vanished in a flash of fire.

All these tales, told in that drowsy undertone with which men talk in the dark, the countenances of the listeners only now and then receiving a casual gleam from the glare of a pipe, sank deep in the mind of Ichabod. He repaid them in kind with large extracts from his invaluable author, Cotton Mather, and added many marvelous events that had taken place in his native State of Connecticut, and fearful sights which he had seen in his nightly walks about Sleepy Hollow.

The revel now gradually broke up. The old farmers gathered together their families in their wagons, and were heard for some time rattling along the hollow roads and over the distant hills. Some of the damsels mounted on pillions behind their favorite swains, and their light-hearted laughter, mingling with the clatter of hoofs, echoed along the silent woodlands, sounding fainter and fainter until they gradually died away -- and the late scene of noise and frolic was all silent and deserted. Ichabod only lingered behind, according to the custom of country lovers, to have a tete-a-tete with the heiress, fully convinced that he was now on the high road to success. What passed at this interview I will not pretend to say, for in fact I do not know. Something, however, I fear me, must have gone wrong, for he certainly sallied forth, after no very great interval, with an air quite desolate and chopfallen. Oh these women! these women! Could that girl have been playing off any of her coquettish tricks? Was her encouragement of the poor pedagogue all a mere sham to secure her conquest of his rival? Heaven only knows, not I! Let it suffice to say, Ichabod stole forth with the air of one who had been sacking a hen roost rather than a fair lady's heart. Without looking to the right or left to notice the scene of rural wealth, on which he had so often gloated, he went straight to the stable, and with several hearty cuffs and kicks roused his steed most uncourteously from the comfortable quarters in which he was soundly sleeping, dreaming of mountains of corn and oats, and whole valleys of timothy and clover.

It was the very witching time of night that Ichabod, heavy-hearted and crestfallen, pursued his travel homeward, along the sides of the lofty hills which rise above Tarry Town, and which he had traversed so cheerily in the afternoon. The hour was as dismal as himself. Far below him, the Tappan Zee spread its dusky and indistinct waste of waters, with here and there the tall mast of a sloop, riding quietly at anchor under the land. In the dead hush of midnight he could even hear the barking of the watchdog from the opposite shore of the Hudson, but it was so vague and faint as only to give an idea of his distance from this faithful companion of man. Now and then, too, the long-drawn crowing of a cock, accidentally awakened, would sound far, far off, from some farmhouse away among the hills -- but it was like a dreaming sound in his ear. No signs of life occurred near him, but occasionally the melancholy chirp of a cricket, or perhaps the guttural twang of a bullfrog, from a neighboring marsh, as if sleeping uncomfortably and turning suddenly in his bed.

All the stories of ghosts and goblins that he had heard in the afternoon now came crowding upon his recollection. The night grew darker and darker; the stars seemed to sink deeper in the sky, and driving clouds occasionally hid them from his sight. He had never felt so lonely and dismal. He was, moreover, approaching the very place where many of the scenes of the ghost stories had been laid. In the center of the road stood an enormous tulip tree, which towered like a giant above all the other trees of the neighborhood and formed a kind of landmark. Its limbs were gnarled and fantastic, large enough to form trunks for ordinary trees, twisting down almost to the earth and rising again into the air. It was connected with the tragical story of the unfortunate Andre, who had been taken prisoner hard by; and was universally known by the name of Major Andre's tree. The common people regarded it with a mixture of respect and superstition, partly out of sympathy for the fate of its ill-starred namesake, and partly from the tales of strange sights and doleful lamentations told concerning it.

As Ichabod approached this fearful tree, he began to whistle; he thought his whistle was answered -- it was but a blast sweeping sharply through the dry branches. As he approached a little nearer, he thought he saw something white hanging in the midst of the tree -- he paused and ceased whistling; but on looking more narrowly, perceived that it was a place where the tree had been scathed by lightning and the white wood laid bare. Suddenly he heard a groan -- his teeth chattered and his knees smote against the saddle; it was but the rubbing of one huge bough upon another as they were swayed about by the breeze. He passed the tree in safety, but new perils lay before him.

About two hundred yards from the tree a small brook crossed the road and ran into a marshy and thickly wooded glen, known by the name of Wiley's swamp. A few rough logs, laid side by side, served for a bridge over this stream. On that side of the road where the brook entered the wood, a group of oaks and chestnuts, matted thick with wild grapevines, threw a cavernous gloom over it. To pass this bridge was the severest trial. It was at this identical spot that the unfortunate Andre was captured, and under the covert of those chestnuts and vines were the sturdy yeomen concealed who surprised him. This has ever since been considered a haunted stream, and fearful are the feelings of the schoolboy who has to pass it alone after dark.

As he approached the stream his heart began to thump: he summoned up, however, all his resolution, gave his horse half a score of kicks in the ribs, and attempted to dash briskly across the bridge; but instead of starting forward, the perverse old animal made a lateral movement and ran broadside against the fence. Ichabod, whose fears increased with the delay, jerked the reins on the other side, and kicked lustily with the contrary foot; it was all in vain; his steed started, it is true, but it was only to plunge to the opposite side of the road into a thicket of brambles and alder bushes. The schoolmaster now bestowed both whip and heel upon the starveling ribs of old Gunpowder, who dashed forward, snuffling and snorting, but came to a stand just by the bridge with a suddenness that had nearly sent his rider sprawling over his head. Just at this moment a plashy tramp by the side of the bridge caught the sensitive ear of Ichabod. In the dark shadow of the grove, on the margin of the brook, he beheld something huge, misshapen, black and towering. It stirred not, but seemed gathered up in the gloom, like some gigantic monster ready to spring upon the traveler.

The hair of the affrighted pedagogue rose upon his head with terror. What was to be done? To turn and fly was now too late; and besides, what chance was there of escaping ghost or goblin, if such it was, which could ride upon the wings of the wind? Summoning up, therefore, a show of courage, he demanded in stammering accents -- "Who are you?" He received no reply. He repeated his demand in a still more agitated voice. Still there was no answer. Once more he cudgeled the sides of the inflexible Gunpowder, and, shutting his eyes, broke forth with involuntary fervor into a psalm tune. Just then the shadowy object of alarm put itself in motion, and, with a scramble and a bound, stood at once in the middle of the road. Though the night was dark and dismal, yet the form of the unknown might now in some degree be ascertained. He appeared to be a horseman of large dimensions, and mounted on a black horse of powerful frame. He made no offer of molestation or sociability, but kept aloof on one side of the road, jogging along on the blind side of old Gunpowder, who had now got over his fright and waywardness.

Ichabod, who had no relish for this strange midnight companion, and bethought himself of the adventure of Brom Bones with the Galloping Hessian, now quickened his steed, in hopes of leaving him behind. The stranger, however, quickened his horse to an equal pace. Ichabod pulled up, and fell into a walk, thinking to lag behind -- the other did the same. His heart began to sink within him; he endeavored to resume his psalm tune, but his parched tongue clove to the roof of his mouth, and he could not utter a stave. There was something in the moody and dogged silence of this pertinacious companion that was mysterious and appalling. It was soon fearfully accounted for. On mounting a rising ground, which brought the figure of his fellow-traveler in relief against the sky, gigantic in height, and muffled in a cloak, Ichabod was horror-struck on perceiving that he was headless! But his horror was still more increased on observing that the head, which should have rested on his shoulders, was carried before him on the pommel of the saddle: his terror rose to desperation; he rained a shower of kicks and blows upon Gunpowder, hoping, by a sudden movement, to give his companion the slip -- but the specter started full jump with him. Away then they dashed, through thick and thin, stones flying and sparks flashing at every bound. Ichabod's flimsy garments fluttered in the air as he stretched his long lank body away over his horse's head, in the eagerness of his flight.

They had now reached the road which turns off to Sleepy

171

Hollow; but Gunpowder, who seemed possessed with a demon, instead of keeping up it, made an opposite turn, and plunged headlong downhill to the left. This road leads through a sandy hollow, shaded by trees for about a quarter of a mile, where it crosses the bridge famous in goblin story, and just beyond swells the green knoll on which stands the whitewashed church.

As yet the panic of the steed had given his unskillful rider an apparent advantage in the chase; but just as he had got halfway through the hollow, the girths of the saddle gave way, and he felt it slipping from under him. He seized it by the pommel and endeavored to hold it firm, but in vain; and had just time to save himself by clasping old Gunpowder around the neck when the saddle fell to the earth, and he heard it trampled under foot by his pursuer. For a moment the terror of Hans Van Ripper's wrath passed across his mind -- for it was his Sunday saddle; but this was no time for petty fears; the goblin was hard on his haunches, and (unskillful rider that he was!) he had much ado to maintain his seat, sometimes slipping on one side, sometimes on the other, and sometimes jolted on the high ridge of his horse's backbone with a violence that he verily feared would cleave him asunder.

An opening in the trees now cheered him with the hopes that the church bridge was at hand. The wavering reflection of a silver star in the bosom of the brook told him that he was not mistaken. He saw the walls of the church dimly glaring under the trees beyond. He recollected the place where Brom Bones's ghostly competitor had disappeared. "If I can but reach that bridge," thought Ichabod, "I am safe." Just then he heard the black steed panting and blowing close behind him; he even fancied that he felt his hot breath. Another convulsive kick in the ribs and old Gunpowder sprang upon the bridge; he thundered over the resounding planks; he gained the opposite side; and now Ichabod cast a look behind to see if his pursuer should vanish, according to rule, in a flash of fire and brimstone. Just then he saw the goblin rising in his stirrups, and in the very act of hurling his head at him. Ichabod endeavored to dodge the horrible missile, but too late. It encountered his cranium with a tremendous crash -- he was tumbled headlong into the dust, and Gunpowder, the black steed, and the goblin rider, passed by like a whirlwind.

The next morning the old horse was found without his saddle, and with the bridle under his feet, soberly cropping the grass at his master's gate. Ichabod did not make his appearance at breakfast -- dinner hour came, but no Ichabod. The boys assembled at the schoolhouse, and strolled idly about the banks of the brook; but no schoolmaster. Hans Van Ripper now began to feel some uneasiness about the fate of poor Ichabod, and his saddle. An inquiry was set on foot, and after diligent investigation they came upon his traces. In one part of the road leading to the church was found the saddle trampled in the dirt; the tracks of horses' hoofs deeply dented in the road, and evidently at furious speed, were traced to the bridge, beyond which, on the bank of a broad part of the brook, where the water ran deep and black, was found the hat of the unfortunate Ichabod, and close beside it a shattered pumpkin.

The brook was searched, but the body of the schoolmaster was not to be discovered. Hans Van Ripper, as executor of his estate, examined the bundle which contained all his worldly effects. They consisted of two shirts and a half, two stocks for the neck, a pair or two of worsted stockings, an old pair of corduroy small clothes, a rusty razor, a book of psalm tunes full of dogs' ears, and a broken pitchpipe. As to the books and furniture of the schoolhouse, they belonged to the community, excepting Cotton Mather's History of Witchcraft, a New England Almanac, and a book of dreams and fortune-telling; in which last was a sheet of foolscap much scribbled and blotted in several fruitless attempts to make a copy of verses in honor of the heiress of Van Tassel. These magic books and the poetic scrawl were forthwith consigned to the flames by Hans Van Ripper, who from that time forward determined to send his children no more to school, observing that he never knew any good come of this same reading and writing. Whatever money the schoolmaster possessed, and he had received his quarter's pay but a day or two before, he must have had about his person at the time of his

173

disappearance.

The mysterious event caused much speculation at the church on the following Sunday. Knots of gazers and gossips were collected in the churchyard, at the bridge, and at the spot where the hat and pumpkin had been found. The stories of Brouwer, of Bones, and a whole budget of others were called to mind; and when they had diligently considered them all and compared them with the symptoms of the present case, they shook their heads and came to the conclusion that Ichabod had been carried off by the galloping Hessian. As he was a bachelor and in nobody's debt, nobody troubled his head any more about him. The school was removed to a different quarter of the hollow, and another pedagogue reigned in his stead.

It is true an old farmer, who had been down to New York on a visit several years after, and from whom this account of the ghostly adventure was received, brought home the intelligence that Ichabod Crane was still alive; that he had left the neighborhood, partly through fear of the goblin and Hans Van Ripper, and partly in mortification at having been suddenly dismissed by the heiress; that he had changed his quarters to a distant part of the country, had kept school and studied law at the same time, had been admitted to the bar, turned politician electioneered, written for the newspapers, and finally had been made a justice of the Ten Pound Court. Brom Bones too, who shortly after his rival's disappearance conducted the blooming Katrina in triumph to the altar, was observed to look exceedingly knowing whenever the story of Ichabod was related, and always burst into a hearty laugh at the mention of the pumpkin, which led some to suspect that he knew more about the matter than he chose to tell.

The old country wives, however, who are the best judges of these matters, maintain to this day that Ichabod was spirited away by supernatural means; and it is a favorite story often told about the neighborhood around the winter evening fire. The bridge became more than ever an object of superstitious awe, and that may be the reason why the road has been altered of late years, so as to

174

approach the church by the border of the millpond. The schoolhouse, being deserted, soon fell to decay, and was reported to be haunted by the ghost of the unfortunate pedagogue; and the plowboy, loitering homeward of a still summer evening, has often fancied his voice at a distance, chanting a melancholy psalm tune among the tranquil solitudes of Sleepy Hollow.

POSTSCRIPT
FOUND IN THE HANDWRITING OF MR. KNICKERBOCKER

The preceding tale is given, almost in the precise words in which I heard it related at a Corporation meeting of the ancient city of Manhattoes, at which were present many of its sagest and most illustrious burghers. The narrator was a pleasant, shabby, gentlemanly old fellow, in pepper-and-salt clothes, with a sadly humorous face, and one whom I strongly suspected of being poor -- he made such efforts to be entertaining. When his story was concluded, there was much laughter and approbation, particularly from two or three deputy aldermen, who had been asleep a greater part of the time. There was, however, one tall, dry-looking old gentleman with beetling eyebrows, who maintained a grave and rather severe face throughout, now and then folding his arms, inclining his head, and looking down upon the floor, as if turning a doubt over in his mind. He was one of your wary men, who never laugh but upon good grounds -- when they have reason and the law on their side. When the mirth of the rest of the company had subsided and silence was restored, he leaned one arm on the elbow of his chair, and, sticking the other akimbo, demanded, with a slight but exceedingly sage motion of the head, and contraction of the brow, what was the moral of the story, and what it went to prove?

The storyteller, who was just putting a glass of wine to his lips, as a refreshment after his toils, paused for a moment, looked at his inquirer with an air of infinite deference, and, lowering the glass slowly to the table, observed that the story was intended most logically to prove:

175

"That there is no situation in life but has its advantages and pleasures -- provided we will but take a joke as we find it.

"That, therefore, he that runs races with goblin troopers is likely to have rough riding of it.

"Ergo, for a country schoolmaster to be refused the hand of a Dutch heiress is a certain step to high preferment in the state."

The cautious old gentleman knit his brows tenfold closer after this explanation, being sorely puzzled by the ratiocination of the syllogism; while, methought, the one in pepper-and-salt eyed him with something of a triumphant leer. At length, he observed, that all this was very well, but still he thought the story a little on the extravagant -- there were one or two points on which he had his doubts.

"Faith, sir," replied the storyteller, "as to that matter, I don't believe one-half of it myself."

D.K.

Name: _____

Reading Selection: _____

1. **What is the author's overall main idea, (central point, or thesis)?**

_____
_____

2. **There are two kinds of supporting details--major and minor. Major details are the primary points that support the main idea and minor details expand major details. List three details and explain how they support the author's primary point?**

Details used	Explanation of how they support the thesis
1.	

Details used	Explanation of how they support the thesis
2.	

Details used	Explanation of how they support the thesis
3.	

3. **The five main patterns of organization are the list of items pattern, the time order pattern, the example pattern, the comparison and/or contrast pattern, and the cause/effect pattern. What is the main pattern of organization used in this article? Explain why it is the main pattern. What other patterns are used? Give some examples.**

Main pattern:

_____

Explain how the main pattern was used:

_____
_____

Write five of the transitions that helped indicate the main pattern of this selection:

_____ _____ _____ _____ _____

Other pattern(s) used:

_____

Explain how the additional pattern(s) were used:

_____
_____

What were some of the transitions that helped you to discover the other patterns?

_____ _____ _____ _____ _____

4. List <u>three</u> facts in the article. <u>Explain why</u> each it is a fact.

	Explanation:
A.) fact:	A.)
B.) fact:	B.)
C.) fact:	C.)

5. List <u>three</u> opinions in the article. <u>Explain why</u> each it is an opinion.

	Explanation:
A.) opinion	A.)
B.) opinion:	B.)
C.) opinion:	C.)

6. What is the author's main purpose in writing this article? Is it to inform, persuade, or entertain? <u>Tell me how you arrived at that conclusion.</u>

_____
_____
_____

7. What is the author's main tone? <u>Explain how you arrived at your answer.</u>

_____
_____
_____

Vocabulary Preview: These words may present challenges when reading. Preview them now, and return to them again if you need to.

Challenging words:	A common definition:
1.	
2.	
3.	
4.	
5.	
6.	
7.	
8.	
9.	
10.	
11.	
12.	
13.	
14.	
15.	
16.	
17.	
18.	
19.	
20.	
21.	
22.	
23.	
24.	
25.	

Vocabulary Preview: These words may present challenges when reading. Preview them now, and return to them again if you need to.

Challenging words: A common definition:

Challenging words:	A common definition:
1.	
2.	
3.	
4.	
5.	
6.	
7.	
8.	
9.	
10.	
11.	
12.	
13.	
14.	
15.	
16.	
17.	
18.	
19.	
20.	
21.	
22.	
23.	
24.	
25.	

Knowledge is Power

Freeman Tilden

NO we don't want no more books!" cried Mr. Caleb Coppins in a tone of belligerent finality.

At the same time he attempted to slam the front door in the enthusiastic face of the young man who stood outside. But the young man, who was no chicken at canvassing, had taken due precautions in expectation of just such an event. He had neatly inserted his foot between the door-casing and the jamb.

"Just a minute, Mr. Coppins," he pleaded.

"Take your foot out of there, or I'll bust it for you!" replied the head of the household.

The young man regarded his victim with something of pity, mingled with subdued joy. He had tamed many a householder like Mr. Coppins, and his thin nose quivered with the excitement of approaching combat.

"You may slam the door, Mr. Coppins," he said earnestly. "You may amputate my foot; but my severed foot will remain inside with you to extol the glory of the eighth wonder of the world -- the `Pan-Continental Encyclopedic Dictionary,' the steam-engine of intellect, the book that will make your name a byword for wisdom and your home the rendezvous of the intellectual elite."

The canvasser's eloquence was not without effect. Mr. Caleb Coppins's set jaw relaxed. He ceased to push against the inserted foot.

"You've got nerve, young feller," he admitted. "Come in! But you can't sell it to me, no matter what it is. We've got books cluttering up the whole house. I can't turn around now without knocking against a book, and I haven't read half of 'em, nor a quarter. And I get the `Agricultural Year-Book' every year from our Congressman."

The canvasser for the "Pan-Continental" followed silently into the musty-smelling parlor, and, at the bidding of the owner, sat down. As Mr. Coppins threw open the door of the seldom-used room the odor of decaying heirlooms nearly gagged the book-agent. With a quick glance he surveyed the chamber of horrors, from the horsehair-covered chairs to the tall bookcase of black walnut, stuffed with dusty volumes that dated from the period when "Vanity Fair" was thought to be a little off color.

I am not surprised to see so many books," said the canvasser, with a subtle feigning of rapture. "I find it worth while to visit only the true lovers of good literature. Ah, Mr. Coppins, how little the average man knows the rare pleasure that we bibliophiles get from our printed treasures!"

The fact was, as the canvasser very well understood, that Mr. Coppins had led him into the parlor not with the idea of doing him honor, but merely to intimidate him -- to prove that the house was already supplied with books.

Mr. Coppins, however, hearing himself described as a bibliophile, and surmising that a bibliophile must be a person of some importance, permitted himself the luxury of remarking that he *was* a bibliophile -- a forty-third-degree bibliophile. In fact, though he was firm in his resolve not to buy any more books just then, he pastured himself on these green and luscious fields of flattery like a half-starved cow from a rocky hillside.

"It's a pleasure to visit a man like you, Mr. Coppins," resumed the canvasser. "Believe me, I appreciate it. My eye sparkled when I saw that bookcase. Maybe you saw it sparkle? Exactly! `Here is a man of parts,' I said to myself. `Here is a man who knows. I would rather talk with a man like this man, and not sell my books, than sell a cart-load of books to the vulgar crowd who cannot appreciate them.'"

The canvasser paused, and Mr. Coppins nodded appreciatively.

"Don't try to tell me that you don't read these books," continued the canvasser. "I admire your modesty, but I know you gorge yourself on them in the long winter evenings. I'll bet you could recite half of them from memory!"

Mr. Coppins, who spent most of the long winter evenings shooting Kelly pool in a stuffy room at the rear of the barber-shop, assented to this indictment with dreamy self-approval.

Suddenly the manner of the canvasser changed. He became violently agitated, for no apparent reason. His eyes took on a gleam of high exultation. He began to pace up and down excitedly in the open space between the what-not and the table full of artificial flowers in glass. Then he stopped and pointed a long finger at Mr. Coppins so suddenly that that gentleman winced.

"You are a man of parts, Mr. Coppins!" he repeated furiously. "Your name was sent to me from the home office in New York -- in New York, understand? You know what books are worth. You know that knowledge is power! You know that a man can rule the world, if he knows enough. Well, then, let me tell you something. You have made one mistake. You have dabbled. Your information has been sound, but spread too thin. I can prove it to you. Shall I?"

Mr. Coppins was fascinated. He nodded feeble assent.

The canvasser's voice became more shrill and cutting. He launched another finger in the direction of the householder's half-scared face.

"Can you tell me," he demanded with emphasis that cut like a Damascene blade, "what was the population of the city of Joliet, Illinois, in 1900? Can you tell me the name of the heaviest element in nature? How much does the earth weigh, down to the fraction of an ounce? Can you go right out into company and tell the names of the opposing generals in the first Punic War? Or what makes sugar crystallize? Or why the sky is blue? Do you know these things?"

"No, I don't," replied Caleb Coppins hoarsely.

"*I* know!" shouted the canvasser victoriously. "I can tell you the colors of the solar spectrum, backward and forward. I can tell you what the interest on one dollar, compounded semiannually at six per cent for a thousand years, would amount to. I can tell you the name of the right-hand man of the Egyptian monarch Rameses II, and the inscription on the tomb of Numa the Lawgiver. What was the first message ever sent over the electric telegraph? Can you tell me that, Mr. Coppins?"

"No, I can't," replied the abashed bibliophile. And then he added, with a ray of wicked hope flickering in his eyes: "Can you?"

"You can bet your best hat I can! The telegraph was invented by Samuel F. B. Morse, and the first message that was flashed over the wire was: `What hath God wrought!'"

Mr. Coppins shrank back from this prodigy of learning, and his hands trembled nervously.

Again the accusing finger shot forth toward the head of the householder.

"What," cried the canvasser, "is telekinesis? What is arteriosclerosis? Who discovered the X-ray? What is the present price of radium per milligram? What is a milligram? What is the coldest place in the United States? Where is Omsk? Who owns the most expensive dog in the world?"

"Calkins the grocer has a darned expensive dog," ventured Mr. Coppins. "He bit a lawyer last week!"

"That is not worthy of you," challenged the canvasser, flushing deeply. "That is trivial. We are dealing in all seriousness with the greater truths. Is there a single book in your excellent library that can tell you the precise nutritive value of the Lima bean?"

"No," admitted Mr. Coppins.

"There you are!" the canvasser shot back swiftly. "You've got lots of books, but if you wanted to find any of these important things in them it would be like hunting for a needle in a haystack. Suppose any one should ask you to give the origin and uses of caoutchouc? Could you do it? No. Could you spell it? No. There is an old Latin proverb, `Scire ubi aliquid invenias magna pars eruditionis est.' You recall it?"

"Perfectly," responded Mr. Coppins, trying to look as much as possible like an ancient Roman.

"Of course you do. You know that it means, `To know where to lay hands on a fact is a great part of learning.' Well, Mr. Coppins, here you are! The `Pan-Continental Encyclopedic

Dictionary' -- the greatest book ever issued from the printing-press -- the book that cost two hundred thousand dollars before a single page was printed -- the book that called for the brains of one thousand of the world's greatest savants. Will you have it in cloth, in buckram, or in limp leather? Don't choose cloth, Mr. Coppins. I beg you won't give way to your first mercenary impulse and choose cloth."

"Why not choose cloth, if it comes cheaper?" asked Mr. Coppins, in one last defensive effort.

"Because," concluded the canvasser, you look, act, and talk like a limp leather man! Sign here -- on this line, please. That's right!"

"How much?" queried Mr. Coppins, after he had committed himself. Already he was breathing more freely, like a man emerging from a trance.

"Ninety-six dollars and fifty cents," was the soothing reply. "The books are worth a thousand dollars to you. One-half the amount down and the rest in monthly instalments{sic}. With these books you can become a walking fund of learning. You can override the village like a Roman conqueror in his triumphal chariot. You can be an oracle, a magnate. Knowledge is power!"

"Ninety-six fifty!" groaned the bibliophile. "I don't know whether to be glad or sorry I didn't shut the door and amputate your foot."

The day will come when you will remember me with a heart full of gratitude, Mr. Coppins. We prepay freight charges. Your check is just as good as your money. Thank you!"

"Durn his hide!" said Caleb Coppins, when the nimble figure had flattened itself against the expanse of distance. "Ninety-six fifty! I feel like I had been mesmerized and robbed. But them books may be wuth it!"

THE "Pan-Continental Encyclopedic Dictionary" came by fast freight. Mr. Coppins bore the treasures to his room, and manufactured a number of reasonable excuses for being in possession of them when Mrs. Coppins should make the inevitable inquiries. He entered the item on his check-stub as "investment," for the benefit of his wife's splendid eyesight; and then he began to absorb knowledge, which is power.

Down in the rear of the barbershop the game of Kelly pool was proceeding with the usual abandon. Mr. Coppins was not present. The twelve ball got the money; the six ball captured the ten-cent stakes; the ivory cue-ball left the table and went into the corner of the room with its accustomed vigor; but Mr. Coppins was not there.

There was a light burning in Mr. Coppins's favorite corner of the house at night. There was a man absorbing the truths of the universe from limp-leather volumes. There was a man accumulating a fund of deathless information. There was a man trying to wring ninety-six dollars and fifty cents' worth of knowledge out of twenty-one volumes that sprang from the brains of one thousand of the world's greatest savants.

The man was Caleb Coppins. The volumes were the "Pan-Continental Encyclopedic Dictionary."

One bright morning Mr. Coppins emerged from his home with an eager look in his eye. He pounded down Main Street until he got as far as Calkins's Cash Grocery, where he met Mr. Hemingway, manager of the canning-factory.

"Morning, Caleb," was the latter's salutation.

Mr. Coppins nodded and then took the other man by the coat-collar and spoke to him crisply.

"What is the temperature of the ocean at a depth of three thousand fathoms?" he asked.

Mr. Hemingway backed off to a safe distance.

"What difference does it make?" he parried.

"How much is a fathom?" continued Mr. Coppins, cocking his head on one side knowingly.

"I don't know."

Mr. Coppins gave a triumphal snort.

"You *ought* to know, Alec," he said. "A man in your position!"

Then he proceeded on his way. He had already picked out

another victim. It was the principal of the high school, on his way to duty.

Before he received that box of books by fast freight Mr. Coppins had always regarded this man -- Sterling Wendell -- with awe. Now he stepped up to him with an air of affable ease and said:

"Mr. Wendell, do you happen to know what is the Algonquin Indian word for summer squash?"

"Why, I don't recall it just this minute," replied the schoolmaster, as if it had slipped from his mind during the last few seconds.

"Perhaps you can tell me what is the chemical symbol for ice-cream?" suggested Mr. Coppins.

"Really, Caleb, I'm a little late for school as it is. I'll be glad to talk over those matters with you some evening. By the way, do *you* know the chemical symbol for ice-cream?"

"I should say I do!" replied Mr. Coppins, hastening onward with a serene heart.

Then Mr. Coppins entered the butcher-shop,

"What can I do for you this morning?" asked the butcher, "Some mighty fine pork just came in."

"Wells," said Caleb sharply, "probably you can tell me the meaning of the word `endosperm'?"

"I'm afraid I can't this morning, Mr. Coppins," replied the butcher reluctantly. "Did you say you'd have a shoulder or a loin roast?"

"No, I didn't. At what temperature would water boil at an altitude of nineteen thousand feet above sea-level?"

Mr. Wells was silent.

"You don't know?" prodded the man of parts.

The butcher shook his head.

"You *ought* to know, in your business," was the commiserating retort.

"I s'pose you know," said the butcher.

"Pretty likely I do!" replied Caleb Coppins, in triumph.

Mr. Coppins visited the bank, and asked to be informed as to the date of the discovery of argon. He also requested information concerning the treatment of anthrax. The cashier threw up his hands and hid behind his card-index.

Mr. Coppins then assailed the clothing-store employees, clamoring for the specific gravity of dried prunes. The employees fell down wofully {sic} on this problem. Mr. Coppins smiled genially.

"*I* know!" he said.

Then he went home. He felt that things were coming his way. He knew that before supper he would be the talk of the village. He felt that there would be a movement on foot to deal with him. He was equally sure that he could be dealt with only at the expense of the dealer.

"The feller was right," ruminated Mr. Coppins. "I've got 'em all thinking. Knowledge is power!"

HIS sudden flare of erudition gained for Mr. Coppins all the popularity of a game-warden. Not since the smallpox epidemic of 1871 had Brookfield been visited by such a pest. The male residents of voting age learned how to disappear around corners or into doorways when they saw Caleb Coppins approaching. The principal of the high school discovered a circuitous route from his home to the school that took only ten minutes longer to travel. Children instinctively shunned this prodigy of information, because Caleb had been reduced, once or twice, to the necessity of holding them up and demanding an answer to the question:

"Which is the longest bridge in the world?"

But the thing that most envenomed Mr. Coppins's former associates of the stuffy room at the rear of the barber-shop was the fact that Caleb had gained no small credit with the feminine part of Brookfield society. Local hostesses who had run short of attractions took him up. He became a lion. The proper thing to do, it developed, was to serve some small refreshments, and then, after the dishes had been spirited away from the parlor, to

188

turn to some harried young male victim and say:

"Mr. Peters, wouldn't you like to ask Mr. Coppins a question?"

In such cases Mr. Coppins would sit back comfortably into the upholstery and cock his head attentively, while Mr. Peters would shrink to the size of a dwarfed child, cough nervously, and ask to be excused from such a wild adventure. Whereupon the forty-third-degree bibliophile would say nonchalantly:

"Oh, go on, Peters, ask me something difficult!"

And then, failing to arouse the fighting spirit of his paltry opponent, Mr. Coppins would ask himself questions and answer them with careless celerity.

Down at the pool-table, one night, Mr. Calkins paused over his shot and remarked to the smoke-embalmed gathering:

"Say, what do you think of this feller Coppins, anyway?"

"I think he's a big bluff," responded a slender youth. "I been thinking it over, and I come to the conclusion that he don't know the answers to half the questions he asks. You notice he always *says* he knows, but he never tells what it is."

"Well, why don't you call his bluff?" asked Mr. Calkins.

The slender youth hitched nervously and replied:

"Aw, what's the use?"

"He's making a great hit with the women," said another man. "You can't go to a party, or anything, these days, without having Coppins rubbed under your nose. We got to do something to that wise gent, or he'll have us back in the peg-top class, or rolling hoop, or something!"

"Where'd he get all that information?" asked some one.

"Gosh, I dunno," replied the grocer. "He never used to know beans; and all of a sudden he launches out as a regular college president!"

"Somebody's got to call his bluff, if he's bluffing. If he isn't, somebody's got to inveigle him into a vacant lot and wallop him," said the grocer.

189

"He's bluffing, all right," affirmed the slender youth.

"Well, who's going to call him?"

The slender youth thought for a moment and then replied:

"What do you say we get young Harold Hussey?"

"Harold Hussey!" echoed half a dozen sneering, raucous voices. "That little shrimp?"

"He may be a shrimp," was the reply; "but what makes him a shrimp? Ain't it because he studies too much? Ain't it because he spends so much time playing the piano and reading magazines and things? Ain't it because his head is so loaded with information that he don't have any time for the pleasures of life? What more do you want?"

"By thunder, he's right!" admitted Calkins. "Harold is the boy. If there's any one in this town that can hand it to Caleb, it's little Harold Hussey. But will he do it? Harold hasn't got the nerve of a chipmunk."

"He'll do it," continued the slender youth, "if you can get him on a subject he's interested in. You just mention music, and you'll see his eyes looking almost human. He knows more about music and musicians than Caleb Coppins could learn in the rest of his lifetime. Me for Harold Hussey!"

"Somebody go get him," said the grocer. "He won't be in bed yet, I guess. It's only quarter of eight. Bring him here to talk it over."

"No, he couldn't stand the atmosphere of this room," objected Wells, the butcher. "He'd faint. We'd better appoint a delegation to wait on Harold and groom him for the occasion. We'll promise him a box of the best fudge if he'll do it."

"There's a great chance coming the night after to-morrow," said the slender youth. "Mrs. Hastings is going to have a surprise party for George Hastings, and everybody's going to turn out to see George try to look surprised. You see, George was the one that thought of the idea. Everybody that comes is supposed to bring something to eat, and it 'll stock up the Hastingses with pie and cake enough for a month, at least. That's the time to spring little Harold Hussey on Coppins."

Half an hour later a couple of the men returned to the barber-shop with the glad news that Harold had consented to propound a number of questions on the momentous occasion. At least, Harold's mother had consented to permit Harold to consent, which was just as good, if not better.

Whereupon a dozen strong men, each shouldering a cue, formed in line and marched around the pool-table, pausing now and then to slap one another on the back and utter some horrible imprecation against Caleb Coppins.

HAROLD HUSSEY had a watery blue eye, tapering fingers, manicured nails, and a slight lisp. It was said that Mrs. Hussey had been disappointed because Harold, her only child, was not a girl. At all events, she had since done all that she could to rectify nature's unfortunate mistake. The only additional shame she could possibly have saddled upon the nineteen-year-old youth would have been to make him wear earrings.

He called his mother "mommy," and she usually referred to him as "my angel." She withheld from Harold the only possibility by which he might have gained some good repute from the rest of his fellows -- she wouldn't let him learn to play ragtime on the piano.

You can't keep a scheme like that quiet in a place like Brookfield. It came to Caleb's ears that Harold Hussey was going to be used against him at the Hastings surprise party, and Mr. Coppins nearly exploded with subdued laughter.

He knew that Harold's knowledge was practically confined to one subject. Now, Mr. Coppins knew nothing about music. But he got to work under his kerosene lamp. He absorbed everything in the "Pan-Continental" that looked as if it might have the taint of harmony. He delved for dates and nourished himself on names.

He arrived at the Hastings home with a glint of vulpine shrewdness in his eyes. He was not perturbed by the surreptitious whispering that went on around him. He picked out the best chair in the crowded rooms, and threw himself into the preliminary course of ice-cream, sandwiches, and cake. Once in a while he cast a withering glance at Harold Hussey, who had been placed opposite to him, and Harold nearly choked upon a mouthful of frosted cake, Mrs. Hussey patted her pride and hope upon his back and spoke soothing words to him.

Mr. Coppins deliberately put away his dishes and drew himself into a dignified attitude of scholastic reflection. Suddenly he remarked:

"I tell you, folks, it's only when a man really begins to learn something that he realizes how much there is to learn. Now, friends, there was a time when I felt pretty sure I knew everything. But I didn't -- not then!"

"I suppose you do now," retorted an untactful guest, out of his heart of writhing hate.

"Oh, no," replied Caleb complacently; "not everything. But little by little I'm accumulating a fund of knowledge. Knowledge is power! I tell you what, it makes a man feel like a real man. It's the little facts that count. How many of you here could tell me, for instance, the length, in American measure, of a Swedish mile? You ought to know, folks. It's important to know those things. How many of you could tell me what language the ancient Egyptians spoke, or who deciphered the first cuneiform inscriptions dug from the great desert near the Nile? You ought to know. Everybody ought to know. Those things are important. Now, *you*," concluded Caleb, pointing at the untactful young man who had opened the subject, "suppose you ask me some question -- any question. Go ahead -- make it a hard one!"

The untactful young man glowered at the enemy and swallowed hard. He took four reefs in his forehead, and the veins stood out on his temples in his effort to think of a poser. Finally he gasped and lay back in his chair, helpless. He couldn't think of a question to save his life!

Mr. Coppins laughed softly and stroked his chin.

"Anybody else?" he said airily.

"Wait a minute!" cried the untactful one, suddenly coming to life with a wild gleam of joy. "Tell us -- tell us -- who discovered the -- monkey-wrench!"

A titter went around the room, and a dozen male mouths

opened with cordial expectation that Caleb Coppins would be crushed to earth. For a second he looked at the ceiling. Then, in a chant that was suspiciously like that of a parrot, he warbled:

"Certainly! The monkey-wrench is not, as some may suppose, an instrument to monkey with; nor indeed has it any connection with the simian tribe. It should really be called a *moncky*-wrench, for it was invented by a Baltimore mechanic named Charles Moncky. Got any other question to ask?"

The youth who propounded the query faded into the background and deftly pulled the background over his naked shame. There was generous applause from the ladies.

"I've got one!" said another brave candidate. "Who discovered glue?"

"Glue!" repeated Mr. Coppins. "Now there's a question! Who discovered glue? I like to have questions like that thrown at me. Glue is an important substance, and everybody should know the answer to that question. Now, glue -- "

Mr. Coppins stopped. Of course, he did not know who discovered glue, and he had not the wit to frame a satisfactory answer to what was in reality an unfair question. It would have been almost as reasonable to inquire who invented bread.

His only hope was a swift diversion.

"Harold," he said, pulling himself together, "you are a musician. I'll bet you anything you don't know all a musician should know about the famous author of `Parsifal.' You don't know how old he was when he died, or where he was born, or where he died, or any of those important data."

"You mean Wagner?" replied Harold.

"I mean Vogner," replied Mr. Coppins, severely precise. "Those who do not know call him Wagner. I call him Vogner, as his fellow countrymen did. The German language is not like our language, you must understand. Now I ask the question, where was that great composer born; and I answer it myself -- he was born in Leipsic, Germany."

"Is that right, Harold?" asked a score of eager voices. "Do you know?"

"That'th right," was the feeble and disappointed reply.

"Leipthic is right."

"You see!" said Mr. Coppins, with a broad smile at the company. "Another important question!" continued Caleb, rubbing his hands gleefully. "A very important question! Where did the great composer die? Shake off the mortal coil, as one might say? I will answer -- at Baireuth. Pronounced `Byroit,' you will please observe."

"Is that right, Harold?" challenged the same palpitating voices.

"No, thir," was the reply. "It ith not!"

"What?" shouted Caleb Coppins menacingly. "Do you mean to tell me, Harold, that I am wrong? Think again, boy, think again!"

"He died in Venice," persisted Harold in feeble exultation and reaching for his mother's hand.

"He did not!" retorted Mr. Coppins.

"He did so," Harold insisted.

"The boy's got you," said Calkins, the grocer. "Give up, Caleb. You're stung!"

"He died in Byroit," said Caleb. "Mind what I tell you. I know!"

"Venice," said Harold Hussey feebly but doggedly.

Mr. Calkins, with a cunning look in his eye, took Harold by the arm and led him aside.

"Are you sure about it, son?" he asked.

"That'th what my book sayth," lisped Harold. "Besides, I know that Wagner died in an old palace on the Grand Canal in Venice."

Calkins turned swiftly upon Caleb. "The boy's got you," he laughed. "Give up; you're stung, Caleb!"

"Nonsense!" said Caleb.

I'll bet you one hundred dollars the boy's right," cried the grocer. "Put up or shut up!"

Mr. Calkins evidently had little idea that Caleb would put up. He paled visibly when Mr. Coppins replied confidently:

"I'll go you!"

"I -- I haven't got that much cash with me," stammered the grocer. "But here are witnesses. I say Harold is right."

"I really hate to take your money," replied Caleb coolly. "It doesn't seem fair, honestly; but you can't blame me. One hundred dollars! I'm your man."

"Really, you mustn't bet money," interrupted Mrs. Hastings, thinking of the dignity of her position as hostess, but secretly hoping that it would be disregarded.

"Let 'em go ahead!" cried the men. "This has been coming to Caleb for a long time." -- -- -- -- -- -- -- -- -- -- -- -- -- -- -- -- -- - - -- -- -- -- -- -- -- -- -- -- -- -- -- -- --

EDITOR'S NOTE -- The erroneous statement that Richard Wagner died at Baireuth is actually to be found in a well-known and usually very accurate work of reference.

"I can prove it by my book," averred Harold. "I'll go right home and get it thith minute."

"Books talk," returned Caleb. "I'll be back in half a jiffy. Then you'll hand me a check for that hundred, Calkins!

TEN awful minutes of suspense passed over the heads of the company. Calkins perspired in a corner and accepted the congratulations of the crowd with a clammy and uncertain hand.

There was a shuffling of feet outside. In another moment Caleb Coppins entered with a large volume bound in limp leather. He opened it and laid it on the table. Then he pressed his finger on a certain spot and threw back his head haughtily. As many as could gather around the evidence regarded the fatal words and groaned. In his corner Mr. Calkins shivered. It was plain:

WAGNER, Richard, German composer, born at Leipsic, 1813; died at Baireuth, 1883.

195

Another scraping of feet outside, and Mrs. Hussey entered with Harold. Harold also had a book. Mr. Coppins deigned to glance at his antagonist's evidence, and his eyebrows lifted somewhat. Harold also had a volume of the "Pan-Continental Encyclopedic Dictionary"!

Then Caleb smiled. All the better -- the same volume to tell the same story!

Mr. Coppins saw Mr. Calkins pounce wolfishly upon Harold's book and whip the pages over. Presently the search ended, and young Hussey pointed to a passage which Mr. Calkins eagerly read. Then the grocer strode toward Caleb with a countenance which somehow made the bibliophile wonder if he had forgotten anything. With a bold front, however, he turned upon Mr. Calkins and asked confidently:

"Is there any other question you'd like to ask me?"

There was a tense moment of hush in the room. A glint of wicked guile that sparked from Calkins's eyes brought a pale spot under each of Caleb's ears. Then he heard these words:

"Yes, Caleb, there are two questions I'd like to ask you. One of them is: Have you seen *this*?"

He planked down before Caleb Harold's volume of the "Pan-Continental" and glued his finger to a pink slip of paper inserted in front of the title-page. Then, in a loud and cheerful voice, he read the following into Caleb's ear:

"ERRATUM -- On page 301 of this volume, under `WAGNER, Richard,' for `died at Baireuth,' read `died at Venice, Italy.'"

Defeated, stricken dumb, Mr. Coppins did not even attempt a reply. After a moment of dead silence the triumphant voice of Mr. Calkins went on:

"Yes, Caleb, and here's the second question -- have you that hundred in your jeans?"

Name: _____

Reading Selection: _____

1. **What is the author's overall main idea, (central point, or thesis)?**

_____
_____

2. **There are two kinds of supporting details--major and minor. Major details are the primary points that support the main idea and minor details expand major details. List three details and explain how they support the author's primary point?**

Details used	Explanation of how they support the thesis
1.	

Details used	Explanation of how they support the thesis
2.	

Details used	Explanation of how they support the thesis
3.	

3. **The five <u>main</u> patterns of organization are the list of items pattern, the time order pattern, the example pattern, the comparison and/or contrast pattern, and the cause/effect pattern. What is the <u>main</u> pattern of organization used in this article? <u>Explain</u> why it is the main pattern. What other patterns are used? Give some examples.**

Main pattern:
_____

Explain how the <u>main pattern</u> was used:
_____
_____

Write five of the transitions that helped indicate the <u>main pattern</u> of this selection:
_____ _____ _____ _____ _____

197

Other pattern(s) used:

_____

Explain how the additional pattern(s) were used:

_____
_____

What were some of the transitions that helped you to discover the other patterns?

_____ _____ _____ _____ _____

4. List <u>three</u> facts in the article. <u>Explain why</u> each it is a fact.

	Explanation:
A.) fact:	A.)
B.) fact:	B.)
C.) fact:	C.)

5. List <u>three</u> opinions in the article. <u>Explain why</u> each it is an opinion.

	Explanation:
A.) opinion	A.)
B.) opinion:	B.)
C.) opinion:	C.)

6. What is the author's main purpose in writing this article? Is it to inform, persuade, or entertain? <u>Tell me how you arrived at that conclusion.</u>

_____
_____
_____

7. What is the author's main tone? <u>Explain how you arrived at your answer.</u>

_____
_____
_____

Appendix

How to Use the Enclosed CD Rom

Step 1: **<u>Carefully</u>** remove the CD from the CD pocket.

Step 2: Insert the CD into your computer. Double click on "My Computer."

Step 3: Double click on the drive that contains the CD as indicated by the name *BNR&SS-Scheg* following that drive letter. This will open the CD.

Step 4: Double click on each of the following folders to install the readers or other information contained within them:

Adobe E-Book Reader: Double click on "Adobe E-Book Reader Installer." This installs the Adobe Reader which will let you view and print any enclosed Adobe files as indicated by PDF on the disk.

PowerPoint Reader: Double click on the "PowerPoint Reader Installer" to install the PowerPoint Reader. This allows you to play the PowerPoint vocabulary games, and view the PowerPoint presentations.

All other folders: Other folders may be added to the disk from one edition to another. Simply click on each folder to open it and then click on the contents to open them.

Some Interesting Topics for Internet Assignments

Topic:	Date Due:	Related Internet Site:
Accutane acne medicine dangers		
Acesulfame - K		
Allergies		
Anhydrous Dextrose		
Anthrax		
Aspartame Dangers		www.dorway.com
Atomic bomb and fluoride waste		
Atrazine (weed killer)		
Bee Die Off		
Benefits of Aloe Vera		
Canola Oil		
Cell phone hazards		
Child Soldiers		
Current Events		
Defective products/Product recalls		www.cpsc.gov
Deformed frogs		
Earthquakes		
Ebola virus		
Echelon spy network/NSA		
European Union/the EURO dollar		
Famous person		
Fertilizers		
Fleas/Ticks/Mites		
Fluoride Poisoning		
Food additives, colorings, flavorings		
Genealogy		
Genetic engineering		
Gulf War Syndrome		
HAARP Technology		
Human Rights abuses		
Irradiation of food		
Love Canal of Niagara Falls, NY		
Luvox and/or SSRI Drugs		
Magazine search		
Microwave ovens dangers		
MTBE gasoline additives		
Museum of Tolerance (Los Angeles)		
Newspaper search		
Pfiesteria		
Rbst or RGBH		
Stem Cell Research		
Sucralose		
Tea Tree Oil		
The Great Chicago Fire		

How to Copy and Paste
From the Internet into MS Word

Highlight the text

• Highlight the text that you want to copy by clicking the left mouse button in front of the 1st word of that text.
• While holding down the left button on your mouse, drag the cursor over the text until all of the text (that you want) is highlighted.
• To copy all of the text, press "Ctrl" and "A".

Copy

• Move the cursor to the copy symbol, or select "copy" from the pull down menu under Edit.

Minimize the Internet article

• Minimize the Internet article by clicking on the minimize symbol at the top right corner of the page.

• It looks like this: ▬

Open MS Word

• Open your Microsoft Word program by double clicking on the Microsoft Word symbol.
• A blank document should appear. If a blank document does not appear, choose "blank document" from the choices given.
• You may use the blank document or prefer to use a template (see next slide).

If Using a Template:

• If you use a template, do the following:
    –1. Click on the open folder.
    –2. At "Look in:" select the down arrow and choose the drive that your disk is in (indicated by a string of numbers following the disk drive letter).
    –3. Click on that drive and then find the download template that you want. Click on that template.

Paste

• Next, place your cursor onto the blank document.
• Click on the paste symbol, or click on "Paste" in the Edit pull down menu.

Your Document Should Now Appear

• Your document should now appear.
    –You can edit it.
    –You can increase, or decrease, the font size.
    –You can check the length of your article.
    –You can print it.
    –You can save it to a disk.

Minimize MS Word and Restore the Internet to Your Screen

• Once you have completed your task, you can minimize (−), or close (**X**) MS Word.
• You can restore your Internet site by moving your cursor to the bottom of the screen, then click on the site information found there on the hidden toolbar (which will appear when your cursor reaches the bottom of the screen). It will then restore you to your Internet site.

Web Sites

Following are some web sites you may wish to explore. The string of letters beginning with **www** is called the Uniform Resource Locator or **URL** (which means address in internet language). The URL goes in the space at the top, which asks for the address, netsite, website, or something referring to the place you want to go. URLs can contain different endings. The most common are: **.com** for commercial sites, **.edu** for education sites, **.org** for organizations, and **.gov** for government sites. Please be aware of these different endings in the addresses below. Always use the correct one to ensure that you get the site that you are looking for.

Computer Information
- Ask Dudley – www.support.dell.com/askdudley
  Technical support in plain English. Type in your question and "Dudley" will call up links that are related to the question.

Education

- Family Education Network – www.familyeducaton.com
  Includes links to thousands of pages on education, information from local school districts, and family and parenting issues.
- Elements of Style – www.columbia.edu/acis/bartleby.strunk
  A style and composition resource for students writing papers.
- Hyperhistory Online – www.hyperhistory.com/online_n2/History_n2/a.html
  Topics include: Civil War, Manet, Tolstoy, Pasteur, and many more.
- Homework Help – www.slco.lib.ut.us/kidhelp.htm
  Research tool for a wide range of grade levels. Topics include: Animals, dinosaurs, mythology, and more.
- The Internet Public Library – www.ipl.org
  Reference library includes Research and Writing Guide, Science Fair Project Guide, and much more.
- Merriam-Webster Online – www.m-w.com
  Dictionary, thesaurus, trivia, and word games.
- Pampers Parenting Institute – www.pampers.com
  Question/Answer – Baby care and child development.
- Atlapedia Online – www.atlapedia.com
  Information on the country of your choice relating to population, exports, currency, history, etc.
- Funk And Wagnalls Multimedia Encyclopedia Online – www.funkandwagnalls.com
  Includes encyclopedia, dictionary, world news, etc.
- Nova Online – www.pbs.org/wgbh/nova
  Covers a variety of topics and has sharp graphics.

Genealogy

- Ellis Island – www.EllisIsland.org Immigration records from 1892-1924
- Cyndi's List – www.cyndislist.com
  Research your family tree.
- The Genealogy Home Page – www.genhomepage.com
  Links to libraries, genealogical societies, mailing lists, etc.
- The Newberry Library – www.newberry.org
  Especially for those looking for families from the New England area of the country

Government

It is important to remember to use **.gov (not .com)** when accessing Government sites. You can use government sites to get the latest government news or to E-Mail your Congressional Representative, Senator, Governor, or even the President and the First Lady.

- United States Government – www.whitehouse.gov
- California Government – www.ca.gov
- United States Senate – www.senate.gov
- House of Representatives – www.house.gov

Health

- American Heart Association National Center – www.amhrt.org
  Topics include: Heart and stroke information, warning signs, health and nutrition tips and medical facts.
- Heart Information Network – www.heartinfo.org
  Topics include: Nutritional information, prevention, and professional responses to consumer questions.
- Healthy Ideas – www.healthyideas.com/weight
  Topics include: Dieting, meal planning, and fitness information.
- Heartpoint – www.heartpoint.com
  Topics include: Weight loss, herbal remedies, pacemakers, low fat recipes, and more.

History

- The African American Mosaic – www.lcweb.loc.gov/exhibits/african/intro.html
  Topics include: Colonization, migration, slavery, and abolition.
- The Civil Rights Timeline – www.wmich.edu/politics/mlk
  Topics include: Brown vs Board of Education, Birmingham, historic speeches and legal decisions.
- Potus – www.ipl.org/ref/POTUS
  History related to the United States Presidents. Includes Presidential Biographies, election results, cabinets and historical documents.
- The Smithsonian – www.si.edu
  Topics too numerous to mention. Includes a "history search engine".

- The History Net – www.historynet.com
  Topics include: American history, World history, Civil War, etc.
- The History Channel – www.histroychannel.com
  This day in history, weekly quizzes, fun and games.
- The History Guy – www.historyguy.com
  Topics include military history and politics. List of wars and conflicts by nation.
- The Martin Luther King Jr. Papers Project At Stanford University – www.stanford.edu/group/king
  Includes some of Dr. King's best known speeches as well as personal letters and a summary of family history.
- African American Web Connection – www.aawc.com/aawc.html
  Topics include: Art, poetry, authors, businesses, churches, entertainment, history, and organizations.
- The Internet African American History Challenge – www.brightmoments.com/blackhistory
  Biographical notes on some of the lesser known figures in African American History.
- National Civil Rights Museum Virtual Tour – www.mecca.org/~crights/cyber.html
  Topics include: Brown vs Board of Education, Montgomery Bus Boycott, Freedom Rides, March on Washington, and many other civil rights landmarks.

Science
- Why Files – www.whyfiles.new.wisc.edu/index.html
  Answers to questions about mad Cow Disease, cloning, asteroids, and other science related topics.
- Planetdiary – www.planetdiary.com
  "Records the events and phenomena that affect Earth and its residents."

Television
- MSNBC – www.msnbc.com
  Up to date news and more
- ABC.com – www.abc.com
  Includes news, sports from ESPN, and ABC soap opera features.
- CBS.com – www.cbs.com
  Local news, weather, and schedules customized to your location by entering your zip code.
- CNN – www.cnn.com
  Online newspaper can be customized to suit your interests.
- NBC.com – www.nbc.com
  Programming schedules, star biographies, chat rooms, and more.

Search Engines

- www.37.com 37 search engines and still growing. Also called www.Megaspyder.com
- www.google.com A good search engine
- www.mamma.comThis meta search engine will search the following seven smaller search engines for your topic. After you get to **mamma.com**, click on **power search** to get all seven.

- Yahoo – www.yahoo.com
- Lycos – www.lycos.com
- Exite – www.exite.com
- Infoseek – www.infoseek.com

- Webcrawler – www.webcrawler.com
- Alta Vista – www.altavista.com
- HotBot – www.hotbot.com

My 10 Favorite Sites

Why I Like This Web Site

- _____

- _____

- _____

- _____

- _____

- _____

- _____

- _____

- _____

- _____

_____

_____

_____

_____

_____

_____

_____

_____

_____

_____

Notes:

_____

_____

_____

_____

_____

_____

_____

_____

A MORE COMPLETE
ESSAY ORGANIZATION   STEP 1
(Outline Page)

_____
Topic

I.   **MAIN IDEA (TOPIC SENTENCE OR THESIS):**

_____

_____

_____

_____

   A _____

      1 _____

         a _____

         b _____

         c _____

      2 _____

         a _____

         b _____

         c _____

      3 _____

         a _____

         b _____

         c _____

_____

_____

_____

B _____

   1 _____

     a _____

     b _____

     c _____

   2 _____

     a _____

     b _____

     c _____

   3 _____

     a _____

     b _____

     c _____

C _____

   1 _____

     a _____

     b _____

     c _____

   2 _____

     a _____

     b _____

     c _____

   3 _____

     a _____

     b _____

     c _____

1 _____

    a _____

    b _____

    c _____

2 _____

    a _____

    b _____

    c _____

3 _____

    a _____

    b _____

    c _____

1 _____

    a _____

    b _____

    c _____

2 _____

    a _____

    b _____

    c _____

3 _____

    a _____

    b _____

    c _____

A MORE COMPLETE PARAGRAPH / ESSAY ORGANIZATION

_____
TOPIC

I. MAIN IDEA (TOPIC SENTENCE OR THESIS):
_____
_____
_____

A. MAJOR SUPPORTING DETAIL (REASON #1):
_____
_____
_____

1) MINOR SUPPORTING DETAIL:
_____
_____
_____

_____a) ARSD: _____
_____b) ARSD: _____
_____c) ARSD: _____

2) MINOR SUPPORTING DETAIL:
_____
_____
_____

_____a) ARSD: _____
_____b) ARSD: _____
_____c) ARSD: _____

3) MINOR SUPPORTING DETAIL:
_____
_____
_____

_____a) ARSD: _____
_____b) ARSD: _____
_____c) ARSD: _____
_____
_____

B. MAJOR SUPPORTING DETAIL (REASON #2):

_____

_____

_____

   1) MINOR SUPPORTING DETAIL:

_____

_____

_____

_____**a) ARSD:** _____

_____**b) ARSD:** _____

_____**c) ARSD:** _____

   2) MINOR SUPPORTING DETAIL:

_____

_____

_____

_____**a) ARSD:** _____

_____**b) ARSD:** _____

_____**c) ARSD:** _____

   3) MINOR SUPPORTING DETAIL:

_____

_____

_____

_____**a) ARSD:** _____

_____**b) ARSD:** _____

_____**c) ARSD:** _____

_____

_____

_____

_____

C. MAJOR SUPPORTING DETAIL (REASON #3):

_____
_____
_____

1) MINOR SUPPORTING DETAIL:

_____
_____
_____

_____a) ARSD: _____

_____b) ARSD: _____

_____c) ARSD: _____

2) MINOR SUPPORTING DETAIL:

_____
_____
_____

_____a) ARSD: _____

_____b) ARSD: _____

_____c) ARSD: _____

3) MINOR SUPPORTING DETAIL:

_____
_____
_____

_____a) ARSD: _____

_____b) ARSD: _____

_____c) ARSD: _____

_____
_____
_____

D. MAJOR SUPPORTING DETAIL (REASON #4):

_____

_____

_____

   1) MINOR SUPPORTING DETAIL:

_____

_____

_____

     a) ARSD: _____

_____

     b) ARSD: _____

_____

     c) ARSD: _____

_____

   2) MINOR SUPPORTING DETAIL:

_____

_____

_____

     a) ARSD: _____

_____

     b) ARSD: _____

_____

     c) ARSD: _____

_____

   3) MINOR SUPPORTING DETAIL:

_____

_____

_____

     a) ARSD: _____

_____

     b) ARSD: _____

_____

     c) ARSD: _____

_____

_____

_____

_____

. MAJOR SUPPORTING DETAIL :

_____

_____

_____

1) MINOR SUPPORTING DETAIL:

_____

_____

_____

_____a) ARSD: _____

_____b) ARSD: _____

_____c) ARSD: _____

2) MINOR SUPPORTING DETAIL:

_____

_____

_____

_____a) ARSD: _____

_____b) ARSD: _____

_____c) ARSD: _____

3) MINOR SUPPORTING DETAIL:

_____

_____

_____

_____a) ARSD: _____

_____b) ARSD: _____

_____c) ARSD: _____

_____

_____

_____

Antibiotic

Credible

Anthrop